Four Plays in One by John Fletcher & Nathan Field

This play was first published in the first Beaumont and Fletcher folio of 1647. However subsequent research has shown that the more likely authors were John Fletcher & Nathan Field.

Field wrote the Induction, The Triumph of Honor, and The Triumph of Love, whilst Fletcher contributed The Triumph of Death and The Triumph of Time.

No exact date for writing has been established and a window of 1608-1613 is thought most probable.

John Fletcher was born in December, 1579 in Rye, Sussex. He was baptised on December 20th.

As can be imagined details of much of his life and career have not survived and, accordingly, only a very brief indication of his life and works can be given.

Young Fletcher appears at the very young age of eleven to have entered Corpus Christi College at Cambridge University in 1591. There are no records that he ever took a degree but there is some small evidence that he was being prepared for a career in the church.

However what is clear is that this was soon abandoned as he joined the stream of people who would leave University and decamp to the more bohemian life of commercial theatre in London.

The upbringing of the now teenage Fletcher and his seven siblings now passed to his paternal uncle, the poet and minor official Giles Fletcher. Giles, who had the patronage of the Earl of Essex may have been a liability rather than an advantage to the young Fletcher. With Essex involved in the failed rebellion against Elizabeth Giles was also tainted.

By 1606 John Fletcher appears to have equipped himself with the talents to become a playwright. Initially this appears to have been for the Children of the Queen's Revels, then performing at the Blackfriars Theatre.

Fletcher's early career was marked by one significant failure; The Faithful Shepherdess, his adaptation of Giovanni Battista Guarini's Il Pastor Fido, which was performed by the Blackfriars Children in 1608.

By 1609, however, he had found his stride. With his collaborator John Beaumont, he wrote Philaster, which became a hit for the King's Men and began a profitable association between Fletcher and that company. Philaster appears also to have begun a trend for tragicomedy.

By the middle of the 1610s, Fletcher's plays had achieved a popularity that rivalled Shakespeare's and cemented the pre-eminence of the King's Men in Jacobean London. After his frequent early collaborator John Beaumont's early death in 1616, Fletcher continued working, both singly and in collaboration, until his own death in 1625. By that time, he had produced, or had been credited with, close to fifty plays.

Nathan Field was born in October 1587 the youngest of seven children, to John and Joan Field.

His father, a Purtian preacher, was very much opposed to London's public entertainments and died a few month's into Nathan's life. The idea, at that point, of Nathan being part of London's theatre scene was a non-starter.

However, after attending St Paul School in the late 1590's he seems, on or around 1600, to have impressed Nathaniel Giles, the master of the Children of the Chapel Royal and also a manager of the new troupe of boy players at Blackfriars Theatre.

Nathan Field would now remain in theatre for the rest of his young life.

He performed in the plays of Jonson, Chapman, Beaumont & Fletcher and other leading dramatists of the day.

Field stayed with the children's company until 1613, his twenty-sixth year. He appears to be the only one of the boy actors of 1600 to remain with the Blackfriars troupe when, in 1609, Philip Rosseter and Robert Keysar assumed control of the company. In this company, he performed in the theatre in Whitefriars and, frequently, at court, in plays such as Beaumont and Fletcher's The Coxcomb.

By this time Field had also added playwright to his talents. His first was A Woman is a Weathercock. This would lead to collaborators with some of the very best and most highly regarded dramatists of their day.

Accounts say that Field was thought of as a great actor but set against this was his bohemian lifestyle which was notoriously wild. The gossip of the day reported that Field was forced to quit the stage after a scandal in 1619 when he fathered a child by the Countess of Argyll.

Nathan Field died at some point between May 1619 and August 1620. By then he was still only in his early thirties but had made a distinctive contribution to the era's theatre.

Index of Contents

Set in Milan, and concerns the Duke and his family – his wife, his sons Gerard and Ferdinand, and Gerard's mistress Violante. A conflict of generations and classes is resolved through two mock deaths and resurrections. Cupid influences the family's recovery from its troubles.

THE TRIUMPH OF DEATH
The third playlet treats the fate of L'Avall, the "lustful Heir" of the Duke of Anjou. L'Avall has put aside his first wife Gabriella to tale a second, Hellena. He encounters a spirit that reproves him for his various sins. L'Avall dies miserable and unforgiven.

THE TRIUMPH OF TIME
The final section features classical deities and anthropomorphic personifications typical of the masque form: Jupiter, Mercury, Time, Desire, Vain Delight, Fames, Poverty, and others. It includes an anti-masque of "Plutus, with a troop of Indians, singing and dancing wildly about him...."

EPILOGUE
Emanuel and Isabella comment on the "triumphs" at their conclusions. Emanuel returns briefly at the end of the piece to complete the frame play.

DRAMATIS PERSONAE
THE INDUCTION
Emmanuel, King of Portugal, & Castile.
Isabella, his Queen.
Lords.
Frigoso, a Courtier   } Spectators of the Play at the
Rinaldo, his acquaintance   } celebration of their Nuptials.
THE TRIUMPH OF HONOUR
Martius, a Roman General.
Valerius, his Brother.
Nicodemus, a cowardly Corporal.
Cornelius, a wittal Sutler.
Captain.

Sophocles, Duke of Athens.
Diana.
Dorigen, Sophocles wife, the example of Chastity.
Florence, Wife to Cornelius.

THE TRIUMPH OF LOVE

Cupid.
Rinaldo, Duke of Milan.
Benvoglio   } Brothers, Lords of
Randulpho   } Milan
Gerard   } Sons of the Duke, supposed
Ferdinand   } lost.
Angelina, Wife to Benvoglio.
Violante, her Daughter, Gerard's Mistriss.
Dorothea, Violante's Attendant.
Cornelia, the obscured Duchess.

THE TRIUMPH OF DEATH

Duke of Anjou.
L'avall, his lustful Heir.
Gentille, a Courtier, Father to Perolot.
Perolot, contracted to Gabriella.
Two Gentlemen.
A Spirit.
Shalloon, servant to L'avall.
Gabriella, the despised wife of L'avall.
Hellena, his second wife.
Casta, Daughter to Gentille.
Maria, a servant attending on Gabriella.

THE TRIUMPH OF TIME

Jupiter.
Mercurie.
Plutus.
Time.
Atropos.
Desire.
Vain Delight.
Bounty.
Poverty.
Honesty.
Simplicity.
Fame.

THE INDUCTION

Enter **DON FRIGOZO** [Noise within]

DON FRIGOZO

Away with those bald-pated Rascals there, their wits are bound up in Vellom, they are not currant here. Down with those City-Gentlemen, &c. Out with those cuckolds I say, and in with their wives at the back door. Worship and place, I am weary of ye, ye lye on my shoulders lik a load of Gold on an Asses back. A man in Authority, is but as a candle in the wind, sooner wasted or blown out, than under a bushel. How now, what's the matter?

Who are you, Sir?

[Enter **RINALDO**.

RINALDO

Who am I, Sir? why, do y' not know me?

DON FRIGOZO

No by my faith do I not.

RINALDO

I am sure we din'd together to day.

DON FRIGOZO

That's all one: as I din'd with you in the City, and as you paid for my dinner there, I do know you, and am beholding to you: But as my mind is since transmigrated into my office, and as you come to Court to have me pay you again, and be beholding to me, I know you not, I know you not.

RINALDO

Nay, but look ye, Sir.

DON FRIGOZO

Pardon me: If you had been my bed-fellow these seven years, and lent me money to buy my place, I must not transgress principles: This very talking with you is an ill example.

RINALDO

Pish, you are too punctual a Courtier, Sir: why, I am a Courtier too, yet never understood the place or name to be so infectious to humanity and manners, as to cast a man into a burning pride and arrogance, for which there is no cure. I am a Courtier, and yet I will know my friends, I tell you.

DON FRIGOZO

And I tell you, you will thrive accordingly, I warrant you.

RINALDO

But hark ye, Signior Frigozo, you shall first understand, I have no friends with me to trouble you.

DON FRIGOZO

Humh: That's a good motive.

RINALDO

Nor to borrow money of you.

DON FRIGOZO

That's an excellent motive.

RINALDO

No my sweet Don, nor to ask what you owe me.

DON FRIGOZO

Why, that is the very motive of motives, why I ought and will know thee: and if I had not wound thee up to this promise, I would not have known thee these fifteen years, no more than the errantst, or most founder'd Castillian that followed our new Queens Carriages a-foot.

RINALDO

Nor for any thing, dear Don, but that you would place me conveniently to see the Play to night.

DON FRIGOZO

That shall I, Signior Rinaldo: but would you had come sooner: you see how full the Scaffolds are, there is scant room for a Lovers thought here. Gentlewomen sit close for shame: Has none of ye a little corner for this Gentleman? I'll place ye, fear not. And how did our brave King of Portugal, Emanuel, bear himself to day? You saw the solemnity of the marriage.

RINALDO

Why, like a fit Husband for so gracious and excellent a Princess, as his worthy mate Isabella, the King of Castiles Daughter doth in her very external lineaments, mixture of colours, and joyning Dove-like behaviour assure her self to be. And I protest (my dear Don) seriously, I can sing prophetically nothing but blessed Hymns, and happy occasions to this sacred union of Portugal and Castile, which have so wisely and mutually conjoyned two such virtuous and beautiful Princes as these are; and in all opinion like to multiply to their very last minute.

DON FRIGOZO

The King is entring: Signior, hover here about, and as soon as the Train is set, clap into me, we'll stand near the State. If you have any Creditors here, they shall renew bonds a Twelvemonth on such a sight: but to touch the pomel of the King's Chair in the sight of a Citizen, is better security for a thousand double Duckets, than three of the best Merchants in Lisbon. Besides, Signior, we will censure, not only the King in the Play here, that Reigns his two hours; but the King himself, that is to rule his life time: Take my counsel: I have one word to say to this noble Assembly, and I am for you.

RINALDO

Your method shall govern me.

DON FRIGOZO

Prologues are bad Huishers before the wise;
Why may not then an Huisher Prologize?
Here's a fair sight, and were ye oftner seen
Thus gather'd here, 'twould please our King and Queen
Upon my conscience, ye are welcome all
To Lisbon, and the Court of Portugal;
Where your fair eyes shall feed on no worse sights

Than preparations made for Kings delights.
We wish to men content, the manliest treasure,
And to the Women, their own wish'd for pleasure.

[Flourish.

[Enter **KING** and **QUEEN**, **EMANUEL** and **ISABELLA**, **LORDS** and **ATTENDANTS**.

EMANUEL
Fair fountain of my life, from whose pure streams
The propagation of two Kingdoms flowes,
Never contention rise in eithers brest,
But contestation whose love shall be best.

ISABELLA
Majestick Ocean, that with plenty feeds
Me, thy poor tributary Rivolet,
Sun of my beauty, that with radiant beams
Dost gild, and dance upon these humble streams,
Curst be my birth-hour, and my ending day,
When back your love-floods I forget to pay:
Or if this brest of mine, your crystall brook,
Ever take other form in, other look
But yours, or ere produce unto your grace
A strange reflection, or anothers face,
But be your love-book clasp'd, open'd to none
But you, nor hold a storie, but your own;
A water fix'd, that ebbs nor floods pursue,
Frozen to all, onely dissolv'd to you.

EMANUEL
O, who shall tel the sweetness of our love
To future times, and not be thought to lye?
I look through this hour like a perspective,
And far off see millions of prosperous seeds,
That our reciprocall affection breeds.
Thus my white rib, close in my brest with me,
Which nought shall tear hence, but mortalitie.

LORDS
Be Kingdoms blest in you, you blest in them.

DON FRIGOZO
Whist, Seignior; my strong imagination shews me
Love (me thinks) bathing in milk, and wine in her cheeks:
O! how she clips him, like a plant of Ivie.

RINALDO

I; Could not you be content to be an Owl in such an ivie-bush, or one of the Oaks of the City to be so clipt?

DON FRIGOZO
Equivocal Don, though I like the clipping well, I could not be content either to be your Owl, or your Ox of the City. The Play begins.

THE TRIUMPH OF HONOUR

[Flourish.

[Enter a **POET** with a garland.

POET PROLOGUE
Low at your sacred feet our poor Muse layes
Her, and her thunder-fearless virdant Bayes.
Four severall Triumphs to your Princely eyes,
Of Honor, Love, Death, and Time do rise
From our approaching subject, which we move
Towards you with fear, since that a sweeter Love,
A brighter Honor, purer Chastitie
March in your brests this day triumphantly,
Then our weak Scenes can show: then how dare we
Present like Apes and Zanies, things that be
Exemplifi'd in you, but that we know,
We ne'r crav'd grace, which you did not bestow?

SCENE I. Before the Walls of Athens

[Enter in triumph with Drums, Trumpets, Colours, **MARTIUS**, **VALERIUS**, **SOPHOCLES** bound, **NICODEMUS**, **CORNELIUS**, **CAPTAINS** and **SOLDIERS**.

MARTIUS
What means proud Sophocles?

SOPHOCLES
To go even with Martius,
And not to follow him like his Officer:
I never waited yet on any man.

MARTIUS
Why poor Athenian Duke, thou art my slave,
My blows have conquerd thee.

SOPHOCLES

Thy slave? proud Martius,
Cato thy countrey-man (whose constancie,
Of all the Romans, I did honor most)
Rip'd himself twice to avoid slavery,
Making himself his own Anatomie.
But look thee Martius, not a vein runs here
From head to foot, but Sophocles would unseame, and
Like a spring garden shoot his scornfull blood
Into their eyes, durst come to tread on him:
As for thy blows, they did not conquer me:
Seven Battailes have I met thee face to face,
And given thee blow for blow, and wound for wound,
And till thou taught'st me, knew not to retire;
Thy sword was then as bold, thy arm as strong;
Thy blows then Martius, cannot conquer me.

VALERIUS

What is it then?

SOPHOCLES

Fortune.

VALERIUS

Why, yet in that
Thou art the worse man, and must follow him.

SOPHOCLES

Young Sir, you erre: If Fortune could be call'd
Or his, or your's, or mine, in good or evill
For any certain space, thou hadst spoke truth:
But she but jests with man, and In mischance
Abhors all constancie, flowting him still
With some small touch of good, or seeming good
Midst of his mischief: which vicissitude
Makes him strait doff his armour, and his fence
He had prepar'd before, to break her strokes.
So from the very Zenith of her wheel,
When she has dandled some choice favorite,
Given him his boons in women, honor, wealth,
And all the various delecacies of earth;
That the fool scorns the gods in his excess,
She whirls, and leaves him at th' Antipodes.

MARTIUS

Art sure we have taken him? Is this Sophocles?
His fettred arms say no; his free soul, I.
This Athens nurseth Arts, as well as Arms.

SOPHOCLES

Nor glory Martius, in this day of thine,
'Tis behind yesterday, but before to morrow:
Who knows what Fortune then will do with thee?
She never yet could make the better man,
The better chance she has: the man that's best
She still contends with, and doth favor least.

MARTIUS

Me thinks a graver thunder then the skies
Breaks from his lips; I am amaz'd to hear,
And Athens words, more then her swords doth fear.

SOPHOCLES

Martius, slave Sophocles, couldst thou acquire
(And did thy Roman gods so love thy prayers,
And solemn sacrifice, to grant thy suit)
To gather all the valour of the Cæsars
Thy Predecessors, and what is to come,
And by their influence fling it on thee now,
Thou couldst not make my mind go less, not pare
With all their swords one virtue from my soul:
How am I vassall'd then? Make such thy slaves,
As dare not keep their goodness past their graves.
Know General, we two are chances on
The die of Fate; now thrown, thy six is up,
And my poor one beneath thee, next thy throw
May set me upmost, and cast thee below.

MARTIUS

Yet will I trie thee more: Calamitie
Is mans true touchstone: Listen insolent Prince,
That dar'st contemn the Master of thy life,
Which I will force here 'fore thy City walls
With barbarous crueltie, and call thy wife
To see it, and then after send her—

SOPHOCLES

Ha, ha, ha.

MARTIUS

And then demolish Athens to the ground,
Depopulate her, fright away her fame,
And leave succession neither stone nor name.

SOPHOCLES

Ha, ha, ha.

MARTIUS
Dost thou deride me?

VALERIUS
Kneel, ask Martius
For mercy, Sophocles, and live happy still.

SOPHOCLES
Kneel, and ask mercie? (Roman) art a god?
I never kneel'd, or begg'd of any else.
Thou art a fool, and I will loose no more
Instructions on thee: now I find thy eares
Are foolish, like thy tongue.

[Solemn Musick.

[Enter **DORIGEN**, **LADYES** bearing a sword.

My Dorigen?
Oh! must she see me bound?

1ST CAPTAIN
There's the first sigh
He breath'd since he was born, I think.

2ND CAPTAIN
Forbear,
All but the Lady his wife.

SOPHOCLES
How my heart chides
The manacles of my hands, that let them not
Embrace my Dorigen.

VALERIUS
Turn but thy face.
And ask thy life of Martius thus, and thou
(With thy fair wife) shalt live; Athens shall stand,
And all her priviledges augmented be.

SOPHOCLES
'Twere better Athens perish'd, and my wife
Which (Romans) I do know a worthie one,
Then Sophocles should shrink of Sophocles,
Commit profane Idolatry, by giving
The reverence due to gods to thee blown man.

MARTIUS
Rough, stubborn Cynick.

SOPHOCLES
Thou art rougher far,
And of a couser wale, fuller of pride,
Less temperate to bear prosperity.
Thou seest my meer neglect hath rais'd in thee
A storm more boystrous then the Oceans,
My virtue, Patience, makes thee vitious.

MARTIUS
Why, fair-ey'd Lady, do you kneel?

DORIGEN
Great Generall,
Victorious, godlike Martius, your poor handmaid
Kneels, for her husband will not, cannot: speaks
Thus humbly, that he may not. Listen Roman,
Thou whose advanced front doth speak thee Roman
To every Nation, and whose deeds assure 't;
Behold a Princess (whose declining head
Like to a drooping lilly after storms
Bowes to thy feet) and playing here the slave,
To keep her husbands greatness unabated:
All which doth make thy Conquest greater: For,
If he be base in ought whom thou hast taken,
Then Martius hath but taken a base prize.
But if this Jewell hold lustre and value,
Martius is richer then in that he hath won.
O make him such a Captive, as thy self
Unto another wouldst, great Captain, be;
Till then, he is no prisoner fit for thee.

MARTIUS
Valerius, here is harmonie would have brought
Old crabbed Saturn to sweet sleep, when Jove
Did first incense him with Rebellion:
Athens doth make women Philosophers,
And sure their children chat the talk of gods.

VALERIUS
Rise beauteous Dorigen.

DORIGEN
Not untill I know
The Generals resolution.

VALERIUS
One soft word
From Sophocles would calm him into tears,
Like gentle showres after tempestuous winds.

DORIGEN
To buy the world, he will not give a word,
A look, a tear, a knee, 'gainst his own judgement,
And the divine composure of his minde:
All which I therefore doe, and here present
This Victors wreathe, this rich Athenian sword,
Trophies of Conquest, which, great Martius, wear,
And be appeas'd: Let Sophocles still live.

MARTIUS
He would not live.

DORIGEN
He would not beg to live.
When he shall so forget, then I begin
To command, Martius; and when he kneels,
Dorigen stands; when he lets fall a tear,
I dry mine eyes, and scorn him.

MARTIUS
Scorn him now then,
Here in the face of Athens, and thy friends.
Self-will'd, stiff Sophocles, prepare to die,
And by that sword thy Lady honor'd me,
With which her self shall follow. Romans, Friends,
Who dares but strike this stroke, shall part with me
Half Athens, and my half of Victorie.

CAPTAIN
By Heaven not we.

NICODEMUS & CORNELIUS
We two will do it, Sir.

SOPHOCLES
Away, ye fish-fac'd Rascals.

VALERIUS
Martius,
To Eclipse this great Eclipse labours thy fame;
Valerius thy Brother shall for once
Turn Executioner: Give me the sword.
Now Sophocles, I'll strike as suddenly

As thou dar'st die.

SOPHOCLES
Thou canst not. And Valerius,
'Tis less dishonour to thee thus to kill me,
Then bid me kneel to Martius: 'tis to murther
The fame of living men, which great ones do;
Their studies strangle, poyson makes away,
The wretched hangman only ends the Play.

VALERIUS
Art thou prepar'd?

SOPHOCLES
Yes.

VALERIUS
Bid thy wife farewell.

SOPHOCLES
No, I will take no leave: My Dorigen,
Yonder above, 'bout Ariadnes Crown
My spirit shall hover for thee; prethee haste.

DORIGEN
Stay Sophocles, with this tie up my sight,
Let not soft nature so transformed be
(And lose her gentler sex'd humanitie)
To make me see my Lord bleed. So, 'tis well:
Never one object underneath the Sun
Will I behold before my Sophocles.
Farewell: now teach the Romans how to die.

MARTIUS
Dost know what 'tis to die?

SOPHOCLES
Thou dost not, Martius,
And therefore not what 'tis to live; to die
Is to begin to live: It is to end
An old stale weary work, and to commence
A newer and a better. 'Tis to leave
Deceitfull knaves for the societie
Of gods and goodness. Thou thy self must part
At last from all thy garlands, pleasures, Triumphs,
And prove thy fortitude, what then 'twill do.

VALERIUS

But ar't not griev'd nor vex'd to leave life thus?

SOPHOCLES
Why should I grieve, or vex for being sent
To them I ever lov'd best? now I'll kneel,
But with my back toward thee; 'tis the last duty
This trunk can doe the gods.

MARTIUS
Strike, strike, Valerius,
Or Martius heart will leap out at his mouth.
This is a man, a woman! Kiss thy Lord,
And live with all the freedome you were wont.
O Love! thou doubly hast afflicted me,
With virtue, and with beauty. Treacherous heart,
My hand shall cast thee quick into my urne,
E're thou transgress this knot of pietie.

VALERIUS
What ails my Brother?

SOPHOCLES
Martius, oh Martius!
Thou now hast found a way to conquer me.

DORIGEN
O star of Rome, what gratitude can speak
Fit words to follow such a deed as this?

MARTIUS
Doth Juno talk, or Dorigen?

VALERIUS
You are observ'd.

MARTIUS
This admirable Duke (Valerius)
With his disdain of Fortune, and of Death,
Captiv'd himself, hath captivated me:
And though my arm hath ta'ne his body here,
His soul hath subjugated Martius soul:
By Romulus, he is all soul, I think;
He hath no flesh, and spirit cannot be gyv'd;
Then we have vanquish'd nothing; he is free,
And Martius walks now in captivitie.

SOPHOCLES
How fares the noble Roman?

MARTIUS
Why?

DORIGEN
Your blood
Is sunk down to your heart, and your bright eyes
Have lost their splendor.

MARTIUS
Baser fires go out,
When the Sun shines on 'em: I am not well,
An Apoplectick fit I use to have
After my heats in war carelesly coold.

SOPHOCLES
Martius shall rest in Athens with his friends,
Till this distemper leave him: O! great Roman,
See Sophocles doe that for thee, he could not
Do for himself, weep. Martius, by the Gods
It grieves me that so brave a soul should suffer
Under the bodies weak infirmitie.
Sweet Lady, take him to thy loving charge,
And let thy care be tender.

DORIGEN
Kingly Sir,
I am your Nurse and servant.

MARTIUS
O deer Lady,
My Mistris, nay my Deity; guide me heaven,
Ten wreathes triumphant Martius will give,
To change a Martius for a Sophocles:
Can't not be done (Valerius) with this boot?
Inseparable affection, ever thus
Colleague with Athens Rome.

DORIGEN
Beat warlike tunes,
Whilest Dorigen thus honors Martius brow
With one victorious wreath more.

SOPHOCLES
And Sophocles
Thus girds his Sword of conquest to his thigh,
Which ne'r be drawn, but cut out Victorie.

LORDS

For ever be it thus.

[Exeunt all but **CRONELIUS** and **NICODEMUS**.

CORNELIUS

Corporall Nicodemus, a word with you.

NICODEMUS

My worthie Sutler Cornelius, it befits not Nicodemus the Roman Officer to parley with a fellow of thy rank: the affairs of the Empire are to be occupied.

CORNELIUS

Let the affaires of the Empire lie a while unoccupied, sweet Nicodemus; I doe require the money at thy hands, which thou doest owe me; and if faire means cannot attain, force of Armes shall accomplish.

NICODEMUS

Put up and live.

CORNELIUS

I have put up too much already, thou Corporall of Concupiscence, for I suspect thou hast dishonored my flock-bed, and with thy foolish Eloquence, and that bewitching face of thine drawn my Wife, the young harlotrie baggage to prostitute herself unto thee. Draw therefore, for thou shalt find thyself a mortall Corporall.

NICODEMUS

Stay thy dead-doing hand, and heare: I will rather descend from my honor, and argue these contumelies with thee, then clutch thee (poor flye) in these eaglet claws of mine: or draw my sword of Fate on a Pesant, a Besognio, a Cocoloch, as thou art. Thou shalt first understand this foolish eloquence, and intolerable beauty of mine (both which, I protest, are meerly naturall) are the gifts of the gods, with which I have neither sent baudy Sonnet, nor amorous glance, or (as the vulgar call it) sheeps eye to thy betrothed Florence.

CORNELIUS

Thou lyest.

NICODEMUS

O gods of Rome, was Nicodemus born
To hear these braveries from a poor provant?
Yet when dogs bark, or when the asses bray,
The lion laughs, not roars, but goes his way.

CORNELIUS

A pox o' your poeticall veine: This versifying my wife has hornified me. Sweet Corporall codshead, no more standing on your punctilio's and punketto's of honor, they are not worth a lowse: the truth is, thou art the Generals Bygamie, that is, his fool, and his knave; thou art miscreant and recreant, not an horse-boy in the Legions, but has beaten thee; thy beginning was knap-sack, and thy ending will be halter-sack.

NICODEMUS

Me thinks I am now Sophocles, the wise, and thou art
Martius, the mad.

CORNELIUS

No more of your tricks good Corporall Letherchops: I say, thou hast dishonour'd me, and since honor now adaies is only repaired by money, pay me, and I am satisfied: Even reckoning keeps long friends.

NICODEMUS

Let us continue friends then, for I have been even with thee a long time; and though I have not paid thee, I have paid thy wife.

CORNELIUS

Flow forth my tears, thou hast deflowred her Tarquin, the Garden of my delight, hedg'd about, in which there was but one bowling Alley for mine owne private procreation, thou hast, like a thief in the night, leap'd the hedge, entred my Alley, and without my privitie, plaid thine owne rubbers.

NICODEMUS

How long shall patience thus securely snore?
Is it my fault, if these attractive eyes,
This budding chin, or rosie-colour'd cheek,
This comely body, and this waxen leg,
Have drawn her into a fools paradise?
By Cupids godhead I do swear (no other)
She's chaster far then Lucrece, her grand-mother;
Pure as glass-window, ere the rider dash it,
Whiter then Ladyes smock, when she did wash it:
For well thou wotst (though now my hearts Commandress)
I once was free, and she but the Camps Landress.

CORNELIUS

I, she then came sweet to me; no part about her but smelt of Soap-suds, like a Dryad out of a wash-bowl. Pray, or pay.

NICODEMUS

Hold.

CORNELIUS

Was thy cheese mouldy, or thy peny-worths small?
Was not thy Ale the mightiest of the earth in Malt,
And thy stope fill'd like a tide: was not thy bed soft, and
Thy Bacon fatter then a dropsie? Come, Sir.

NICODEMUS

Mars then inspire me with the fencing skill
Of our Tragedian Actors. Honor pricks;
And Sutler, now I come with thwacks and thwicks.
Grant us one crush, one pass, and now a high, Cavalto fall:

Then up again, now down again, yet do no harm at all.

[Enter **WIFE**.

WIFE
O that ever I was born: why Gent?

CORNELIUS
Messaline of Rome, away, disloyal Concubine: I will be deafer to thee, then thou art to others: I will have my hundred drachma's he owes me, thou arrant whore.

WIFE
I know he is an hundred drachmaes o'the score; but what o' that? no bloodshed, sweet Cornelius. O my heart; o' my conscience 't is faln thorow the bottom of my bellie. O my sweet Didimus, if either of ye miskil one another, what will become of poor Florence? Pacifie your selves, I pray.

CORNELIUS
Go to, my heart is not stone; I am not marble: drie your eyes, Florence; the scurvie apes-face knows my blinde side well enough: leave your puling; will this content ye? let him tast thy nether lip, which in signe of amitie I thus take off again: go thy ways, and provide the Cows udder.

NICODEMUS
Lilie of Concord. And now, honest Sutler, since I have had proof as well of thy good nature, as of thy wives before, I will acquaint thee with a project shall fully satisfie thee for thy debt. Thou shalt understand I am shortly to be knighted.

CORNELIUS
The devil thou art.

NICODEMUS
Renounce me else; for the sustenance of which Worship (which Worship many times wants sustenance) I have here the Generals grant to have the leading of two hundred men.

CORNELIUS
You jest, you jest.

NICODEMUS
Refuse me else to the pit.

CORNELIUS
Mercie on us: ha you not forgot your self? by your swearing you should be knighted already.

NICODEMUS
Damn me, Sir, here's his hand, read it.

CORNELIUS
Alas, I cannot.

NICODEMUS

I know that.

It has pleas'd the General to look upon my service. Now, Sir, shall you joyn with me in petitioning for fifty men more, in regard of my arrearages to you; which if granted, I will bestow the whole profit of those fifty men on thee and thine heirs for ever, till Atropos do cut this simple thred.

CORNELIUS

No more, dear Corporal, Sir Nicodemus, that shall be, I cry your wishes mercie: I am your servant body and goods, moveables and immoveables; use my house, use my wife, use me, abuse me, do what you list.

NICODEMUS

A figment is a candid lye: this is an old Pass. Mark what follows.

[Exeunt.

SCENE II

A Rocky View Before the City

[Enter **MARTIUS** and **TWO CAPTAINS**.

MARTIUS

Pray leave me: you are Romans, honest men,
Keep me not company, I am turn'd knave,
Have lost my fame and nature. Athens, Athens,
This Dorigen is thy Palladium:
He that will sack thee, must betray her first,
Whose words wound deeper than her husbands sword;
Her eyes make captive still the Conqueror,
And here they keep her only to that end.
O subtill devil, what a golden ball
Did tempt, when thou didst cast her in my way!
Why, foolish Sophocles, broughtst thou not to field
Thy Lady, that thou mightst have overcome?
Martius had kneel'd, and yielded all his wreathes
That hang like Jewels on the seven-fold hill,
And bid Rome, send him out to fight with men,
(For that she knew he durst) and not 'gainst Fate
Or Deities, what mortal conquers them?
Insatiate Julius, when his Victories
Had run ore half the world, had he met her,
There he had stopt the legend of his deeds,
Laid by his Arms, been overcome himself,
And let her vanquish th' other half. And fame
Made beauteous Dorigen, the greater name.

Shall I thus fall? I will not; no, my tears
Cast on my heart, shall quench these lawless fires:
He conquers best, conquers his lewd desires.

[Enter **DORIGEN**, with **LADYES**.

DORIGEN
Great Sir, my Lord commands me visit you,
And thinks your retir'd melancholy proceeds
From some distast of worthless entertainment.
Will't please you take your chamber? how d'ye do, Sir?

MARTIUS
Lost, lost again; the wild rage of my blood
Doth Ocean-like oreflow the shallow shore
Of my weak virtue: my desire's a vane,
That the least breath from her turns every way.

DORIGEN
What says my Lord?

MARTIUS
Dismiss your women, pray,
And I'll reveal my grief.

DORIGEN
Leave me.

MARTIUS
Long tales of love (whilst love it self
Might be enjoyed) are languishing delays.
There is a secret strange lies in my brest,
I will partake wi' you, which much concerns
Your Lord, your self, and me. Oh!

DORIGEN
Strange secrets, Sir,
Should not be made so cheap to strangers: yet,
If your strange secret do no lower lie
Then in your brest, discover it.

MARTIUS
I will.
Oh! can you not see it, Lady, in my sighs?

DORIGEN
Sighs none can paint, and therefore who can see?

MARTIUS

Scorn me not, Dorigen, with mocks: Alcides,
That master'd monsters, was by beautie tam'd,
Omphale smil'd his club out of his hand,
And made him spin her smocks. O sweet, I love you,
And I love Sophocles: I must enjoy you,
And yet I would not injure him.

DORIGEN

Let go;
You hurt me, Sir: fare well. Stay, is this Martius?
I will not tell my Lord; he'll swear I lye.
Doubt my fidelitie, before thy honor.
How hast thou vex'd the gods, that they would let thee
Thus violate friendship, hospitalitie,
And all the bounds of sacred pietie?
Sure thou but tri'st me out of love to him,
And wouldst reject me, if I did consent.
O Martius, Martius, wouldst thou in one minute,
Blast all thy Laurels, which so many years
Thou hast been purchasing with blood and sweat?
Hath Dorigen never been written, read,
Without the epithet of chast, chast Dorigen?
And wouldst thou fall upon her chastitie,
Like a black drop of ink, to blot it out?
When men shall read the records of thy valour,
Thy hitherto-brave virtue, and approach
(Highly content yet) to this foul assault
Included in this leaf, this ominous leaf,
They shall throw down the Book, and read no more,
Though the best deeds ensue, and all conclude,
That ravell'd the whole story, whose sound heart
(Which should have been) prov'd the most leprous part.

MARTIUS

O! thou confut'st divinely, and thy words
Do fall like rods upon me; but they have
Such silken lines, and silver hooks, that I
Am faster snar'd: my love has ta'en such hold,
That (like two wrestlers) though thou stronger be,
And hast cast me, I hope to pull thee after.
I must, or perish.

DORIGEN

Perish, Martius, then;
For I here vow unto the gods, These rocks,
These rocks we see so fix'd, shall be removed,
Made champion field, ere I so impious prove,

To stain my Lords bed with adulterous love.

[Enter **VALERIUS**.

VALERIUS
The gods protect fair Dorigen.

DORIGEN
Amen,
From all you wolvish Romanes.

[Exit.

VALERIUS
Ha? what's this?
Still, brother, in your moods? O then my doubts
Are truths. Have at it: I must try a way
To be resolv'd.

MARTIUS
How strangely dost thou look! what ailst thou?

VALERIUS
What ailst thou?

MARTIUS
Why, I 'm mad.

VALERIUS
Why, I am madder. Martius, draw thy sword,
And lop a villain from the earth; for if
Thou wilt not, on some tree about this place
I'll hang my self; Valerius shall not live
To wound his brothers honor, stain his Countrey,
And branded with ingratitude to all times.

MARTIUS
For what can all this be?

VALERIUS
I am in love.

MARTIUS
Why so am I. With whom? ha?

VALERIUS
Dorigen.

MARTIUS
With Dorigen? how dost thou love her? speak.

VALERIUS
Even to the height of lust; and I must have her or else I die.

MARTIUS
Thou shalt, thou daring Traitor.
On all the confines I have rid my horse,
Was there no other woman for thy choice
But Dorigen? Why, villain, she is mine:
She makes me pine thus, sullen, mad, and fool;
'T is I must have her, or I die.

VALERIUS
O all ye gods,
With mercy look on this declining rock
Of valour, and of virtue; breed not up
(From infancie) in honor, to full man,
As you have done him, to destroy: here, strike;
For I have onely search'd thy wound: dispatch;
Far, far be such love from Valerius,
So far he scorns to live to be call'd brother
By him that dares own such folly and such vice.

MARTIUS
'T is truth thou speak'st; but I do hate it: peace,
If heaven will snatch my sword out of my hand,
And put a rattle in it, what can I do?
He that is destin'd to be odious
In his old age, must undergo his fate.

[Enter **CORNELIUS** and **NICODEMUS**.

CORNELIUS
If you do not back me, I shall never do't.

NICODEMUS
I warrant you.

CORNELIUS
Humh, humh: Sir; my Lord, my Lord.

MARTIUS
Hah? what's the matter?

CORNELIUS
Humh; concerning the odd fifty, my Lord, and 't please your

Generality, his Worship, Sir Nicodemus.

MARTIUS
What's here? a Pass? you would for Rome? you lubbers, doth one days laziness make ye covet home? away, ye boarish rogues; ye dogs, away.

[Enter **WIFE**.

WIFE
Oh, oh, oh:
How now man, are you satisfi'd?

CORNELIUS
Ay, ay, ay: a pox o' your Corporal; I 'm paid soundly, I was never better paid in all my life.

WIFE
Marry the gods blessing on his honors heart: you have done a charitable deed, Sir, many more such may you live to do, Sir: the gods keep you, Sir, the gods protect you.

[Exit.

MARTIUS
These peasants mock me sure (Valerius)
Forgive my dotage, see my ashes urn'd,
And tell fair Dorigen, (she that but now
Left me with this harsh vow, Sooner these rocks
Should be remov'd, then she would yield) that I
Was yet so loving, on her gift to die.

VALERIUS
O Jupiter forbid it, Sir, and grant
This my device may certifie thy mind:
You are my brother, nor must perish thus:
Be comforted: think you fair Dorigen
Would yield your wishes, if these envious rocks
By skill could be remov'd, or by fallacie
She made believe so?

MARTIUS
Why, she could not chuse;
The Athenians are religious in their vows,
Above all nations.

VALERIUS
Soft, down yonder hill
The Lady comes this way, once more to trie her,
If she persist in obstinacie: by my skill
Learn'd from the old Caldean was my Tutor,

Who train'd me in the Mathematicks, I will
So dazle and delude her sight, that she
Shall think this great impossibilitie
Effected by some supernatural means.
Be confident; this engine shall at least,
Till the gods better order, still this brest.

[Exit **VALERIUS**.

MARTIUS
O my best brother, go; and for reward,
Chuse any part o'th' world, I'll give it thee.
O little Rome, men say thou art a god;
Thou mightst have got a fitter fool then I.

[Enter **DORIGEN**.

DORIGEN
Art thou there, Basilisk? remove thine eyes,
For I'm sick to death with thy infection.

MARTIUS
Yet, yet have mercy on me; save him, Lady,
Whose single arm defends all Rome, whose mercie
Hath sav'd thy husband's and thy life.

DORIGEN
To spoil
Our fame and honors? no, my vow is fixt,
And stands, as constant as these stones do, still.

MARTIUS
Then pitie me, ye gods; you onely may
Move her, by tearing these firm stones a way.

[Solemn musick.

[A mist ariseth, the rocks remove.

[Enter **VALERIUS** like Mercury, singing.

VALERIUS
Martius rejoyce, Jove sends me from above,
His Messenger, to cure thy desperate love;
To shew rash vows cannot binde destinie:
Lady, behold, the rocks transplanted be.
Hard-hearted Dorigen, yield, lest for contempt,
They fix thee here a rock, whence they 're exempt.

DORIGEN

What strange delusion's this? what Sorcery
Affrights me with these apparitions?
My colder Chastity's nigh turn'd to death.
Hence, lewd Magician; dar'st thou make the gods
Bawds to thy lust; will they do miracles
To further evil? or do they love it now?
Know, if they dare do so, I dare hate them,
And will no longer serve 'em. Jupiter,
Thy golden showr, nor thy snow-white Swan,
Had I been Læda, or bright Danae,
Had bought mine honor. Turn me into stone
For being good, and blush when thou hast done.

[Exit **DORIGEN**.

[Enter **VALERIUS**.

MARTIUS

O my Valerius, all yet will not do;
Unless I could so draw mine honestie
Down to the lees to be a ravisher;
She calls me witch, and villain.

VALERIUS

Patience, Sir,
The gods will punish perjury. Let her breathe
And ruminate on this strange sight. Time decays
The strongest fairest buildings we can finde;
But still Diana, fortifie her minde.

[Exeunt.

SCENE III

Athens. A Room in the House of Sophocles

[Enter **SOPHOCLES** and **DORIGEN**.

SOPHOCLES

Weep not bright Dorigen; for thou hast stood
Constant and chaste (it seems 'gainst gods and men)
When rocks and mountains were remov'd. These wonders
Do stupifie my senses. Martius,
This is inhumane: was thy sickness lust?

Yet were this truth, why weeps she? Jealous soul,
What dost thou thus suggest? Vows, Magick, Rocks?
Fine tales, and tears. She ne'er complain'd before.
I bade her visit him; she often did,
Had many opportunities. Humh, 'tis naught: O!
No way but this. Come, weep no more, I have ponder'd
This miracle: the anger of the gods,
Thy vow, my love to thee, and Martius:
He must not perish, nor thou be forsworn,
Lest worse fates follow us; Go, keep thy oath:
For chaste, and whore, are words of equal length:
But let not Martius know that I consent,
O! I'm pull'd in pieces.

DORIGEN
I? say you so?
I'll meet you in your path. O wretched men!
With all your valour and your learning, bubbles.
Forgive me, Sophocles. Yet why kneel I
For pardon, having been but over-diligent,
Like an obedient servant, antedating
My Lords command? Sir, I have often, and already given
This bosom up to his embraces, and
Am proud that my dear Lord is pleas'd with it;
Whose gentle honorable minde I see
Participates even all, his wife and all,
Unto his friend. You are sad, Sir. Martius loves me,
And I love Martius with such ardencie,
As never married couple could: I must
Attend him now. My Lord, when you have need
To use your own wife, pray Sir send for me;
Till then, make use of your Philosophie.

[Exit.

SOPHOCLES
Stay, Dorigen: O me, inquisitive fool!
Thou that didst order this congested heap
When it was Chaos, 'twixt thy spacious palms
Forming it to this vast rotundie;
Dissolve it now; shuffle the elements,
That no one proper by it self may stand:
Let the sea quench the sun, and in that instant
The sun drink up the sea: day, ne'er come down,
To light me to those deeds that must be done.

[Exit.

The Roman Camp Before the City

[Drums and Colours.

[Enter **MARTIUS**, **VALERIUS**, **CAPTAINS** and **SOLDIERS**, at one door, and **DORIGEN** with **LADYES**, at another.

DORIGEN
Hail, General of Rome; from Sophocles
That honors Martius, Dorigen presents
Her self to be dishonour'd: do thy will;
For Sophocles commands me to obey.
Come, violate all rules of holiness,
And rend the consecrated knot of love.

MARTIUS
Never, Valerius, was I blest till now:
Behold the end of all my weary steps,
The prize of all my Battels: leave us all;
Leave us as quick as thought. Thus joy begin,
In zealous love a minutes loss is sin.

VALERIUS
Can Martius be so vile? or Dorigen?

DORIGEN
Stay, stay, and monster, keep thou further of;
I thought thy brave soul would have much, much loath'd
To have gone on still on such terms as this.
See, thou ungrateful, since thy desperate lust
Nothing can cure but death, I'll die for thee,
Whilst my chaste name lives to posterity.

[Offers to kill herself.

MARTIUS
Live, live, thou Angel of thy sex: forgive,
Till by those golden tresses thou be'st snatch'd
Alive to Heaven: for thy corruption's
So little, that it cannot suffer death.
Was ever such a woman? O my mirror!
How perfectly thou shew'st me all my faults,
Which now I hate, and when I next attempt thee,
Let all the fires in the Zodiak

Drop on this cursed head.

ALL
O blest event!

DORIGEN
Rise like the sun again in all his glory,
After a dark Eclipse.

MARTIUS
Never without a pardon.

[Enter **SOPHOCLES**, and two or three with him.

DORIGEN
Sir, you have forgiven your self.

SOPHOCLES
Behold their impudence: are my words just?
Unthankful man, viper to Arms, and Rome
Thy natural mother; have I warm'd thee here
To corrode ev'n my heart? Martius, prepare
To kill me, or be kill'd.

MARTIUS
Why Sophocles?
Then prethee kill me; I deserve it highly;
For I have both transgress'd 'gainst men, and gods;
But am repentant now, and in best case
To uncase my soul of this oppressing flesh;
Which, though (Gods witness) nev'r was actually
Injurious to thy wife and thee, yet 't was
Her goodness that restrain'd and held me now:
But take my life, dear friend, for my intent,
Or else forgive it.

VALERIUS
By the gods of Athens,
These words are true, and all direct again.

SOPHOCLES
Pardon me, Dorigen.

MARTIUS
Forgive me, Sophocles,
And Dorigen too, and every one that 's good.

DORIGEN

Rise, noble Roman, belov'd Sophocles,
Take to thy brest thy friend.

MARTIUS
And to thy heart
Thy matchless wife: Heaven has not stuff enough
To make another such: for if it could,
Martius would marry too. For thy blest sake
(O thou infinitie of excellence)
Henceforth in mens discourse Rome shall not take
The wall of Athens, as 'tofore. But when
In their fair honors we to speak do come,
We'll say 'T was so in Athens, and in Rome.

[Exeunt in pomp.

[**DIANA** descends.

DIANA
Honor set ope thy gates, and with thee bring
My servant and thy friend, fair Dorigen:
Let her triumph, with her, her Lord, and friend,
Who, though misled, still honor was their end.

[Flourish.

[Enter the Shew of Honors Triumph; a great flourish of Trumpets and Drums within; Then enter a noise of Trumpets sounding cheerfully. Then follows an armed **KNIGHT** bearing a Crimson Banneret in hand, with the inscription Valour: by his side a **LADY**, bearing a Watchet Banneret, the inscription Clemencie: next **MARTIUS** and **SOPHOCLES** with Coronets. Next, **TWO LADIES**, one bearing a white Banneret, the inscription Chastlty: the other a black, the inscription Constancie. Then **DORIGEN** crown'd. Last, a Chariot drawn by **TWO MOORS**, in it a **PERSON** crown'd, with a Scepter: on the top, in an antick Scutcheon, is written Honor. As they pass over, **DIANA** ascends.

RINALDO
How like you it?

DON FRIGOZO
Rarely; so well, I would they would do it again. How many of our wives now adays would deserve to triumph in such a Chariot?

RINALDO
That's all one; you see they triumph in Caroches.

DON FRIGOZO
That they do, by the mass; but not all neither; many of them are content with Carts. But Seignior, I have now found out a great absurditie i'faith.

RINALDO
What was 't?

DON FRIGOZO
The Prologue presenting four Triumphs, made but three legs to the King: a three-legged Prologue, 't was monstrous.

RINALDO
'T had been more monstrous to have had a four-legg'd one.
Peace, the King speaks.

EMANUEL
Here was a woman, Isabel.

ISABELLA
I, my Lord,
But that she told a lye to vex her husband;
Therein she fail'd.

EMANUEL
She serv'd him well enough;
He that was so much man, yet would be cast
To jealousie for her integrity.
This teacheth us, the passion of love
Can fight with Soldiers, and with Scholars too.

ISABELLA
In Martius, clemencie and valour shown,
In the other, courage and humanitie;
And therefore in the Triumph they were usher'd
By clemencie and valour.

EMANUEL
Rightly observ'd,
As she by chastitie and constancie;
What hurt's now in a Play, against which some rail
So vehemently? thou and I, my love,
Make excellent use methinks: I learn to be
A lawful lover void of jealousie,
And thou a constant wife. Sweet Poetry's
A flower, where men, like Bees and Spiders, may
Bear poison, or else sweets and Wax away.
Be venom-drawing Spiders they that will;
I'll be the Bee, and suck the honey still.

[Flourish.

[**CUPID** descends.

CUPID
Stay, clouds, ye rack too fast: bright Phœbus see,
Honor has triumph'd with fair Chastity:
Give Love now leave, in purity to shew
Unchaste affections flie not from his bowe.
Produce the sweet example of your youth.
Whilst I provide a Triumph for your Truth.

[Flourish.

THE TRIUMPH OF LOVE

SCENE I

Milan. A Room in Benvoglio's House

[Enter **VIOLANTA**, with **CHILD** and **GERRARD**.

VIOLANTA
Why does my Gerrard grieve?

GERRARD
O my sweet Mistris,
'Tis not life (which by our Milain law
My fact hath forfeited) makes me thus pensive;
That I would lose to save the little finger
Of this your noble burthen, from least hurt,
Because your blood is in't. But since your love
Made poor incompatible me the parent,
(Being we are not married) your dear blood
Falls under the same cruel penalty;
And can Heaven think fit ye die for me?
For Heavens sake say I ravisht you, I'll swear it,
To keep your life, and repute unstain'd.

VIOLANTA
O Gerrard, th' art my life and faculties:
And if I lose thee, I'll not keep mine own;
The thought of whom, sweetens all miseries.
Wouldst have me murder thee beyond thy death?
Unjustly scandal thee with ravishment?
It was so far from rape, that Heaven doth know,
If ever the first Lovers, ere they fell,
Knew simply in the state of innocence,
Such was this act, this, that doth ask no blush.

GERRARD

O! but my rarest Violanta, when
My Lord Randulpho brother to your father,
Shall understand this, how will he exclaim,
That my poor Aunt, and me, which his free alms
Hath nurs'd, since Millain by the Duke of Mantua
(Who now usurps it) was surpriz'd? that time
My father and my mother were both slain,
With my Aunts husband, as she says, their states
Despoil'd and seiz'd; 'tis past my memory,
But thus she told me: onely thus I know,
Since I could understand, your honor'd Uncle
Hath given me all the liberal education,
That his own son might look for, had he one;
Now will he say, Dost thou requite me thus?
O! the thought kills me.

VIOLANTA

Gentle, gentle Gerrard,
Be cheer'd, and hope the best. My mother, father,
And uncle love me most indulgently,
Being the onely branch of all their stocks:
But neither they, nor he thou wouldst not grieve
With this unwelcom news, shall ever hear
Violanta's tongue reveal, much less accuse
Gerrard to be the father of his own;
I'll rather silent die, that thou maist live
To see thy little of-spring grow and thrive.

[Enter **DOROTHEA**.

DOROTHEA

Mistris, away, your Lord and father seeks you;
I'll convey Gerrard out at the back door;
He has found a husband for you, and insults
In his invention, little thinking you
Have made your own choice, and possest him too.

VIOLANTA

A husband? 't must be Gerrard, or my death.
Fare well; be onely true unto thy self,
And know Heavens goodness shall prevented be,
Ere worthiest Gerrard suffer harm for me.

GERRARD

Fare well, my life and soul. Aunt, to your counsel
I flee for aid. O unexpressible love! thou art

An undigested heap of mixt extremes,
Whose pangs are wakings, and whose pleasures dreams.

[Exeunt.

Another in the Same

[Enter **BENVOGLIO, ANGELINA, FERDINAND**.

BENVOGLIO
My Angelina, never didst thou yet
So please me, as in this consent; and yet
Thou hast pleas'd me well, I swear, old wench: ha, ha.
Ferdinand, she's thine own; thou'st have her, boy,
Ask thy good Lady else.

FERDINAND
Whom shall I have, Sir?

BENVOGLIO
Whom d' ye think, ifaith?

ANGELINA
Ghess.

FERDINAND
Noble Madam,
I may hope (prompted by shallow merit)
Through your profound grace, for your chamber-maid.

BENVOGLIO
How 's that? how 's that?

FERDINAND
Her chamber-maid, my Lord.

BENVOGLIO
Her chamber-pot, my Lord. You modest ass,
Thou never shew'dst thy self an ass till now.
'Fore Heaven I am angrie with thee. Sirha, sirha,
This whitmeat spirit's not yours, legitimate,
Advance your hope, and 't please you: ghess again.

ANGELINA

And let your thoughts flee higher: aim them right;
Sir, you may hit, you have the fairest white.

FERDINAND
If I may be so bold then, my good Lord,
Your favour doth encourage me to aspire
To catch my Ladyes Gentlewoman.

BENVOGLIO
Where?
Where would you catch her?
Do you know my daughter Violanta, Sir?

ANGELINA
Well said: no more about the bush.

FERDINAND
My good Lord,
I have gaz'd on Violanta, and the stars,
Whose Heavenly influence I admir'd, not knew,
Nor ever was so sinful to believe
I might attain 't.

BENVOGLIO
Now you are an ass again;
For if thou ne'er attain'st, 't is onely long
Of that faint heart of thine, which never did it.
She is your Lords heir, mine, Benvoglio's heir,
My brothers too, Randulpho's; her descent
Not behinde any of the Millanois.
And Ferdinand, although thy parentage
Be unknown, thou know'st that I have bred thee up
From five yeers old, and (do not blush to hear it)
Have found thy wisdom, trust, and fair success
So full in all my affairs, that I am fitter
To call thee Master, then thou me thy Lord.
Thou canst not be but sprung of gentlest blood;
Thy minde shines thorow thee, like the radiant sun,
Although thy body be a beauteous cloud.
Come, seriously this is no flatterie,
And well thou know'st it, though thy modest blood
Rise like the morning in thy cheek to hear 't.
Sir, I can speak in earnest: Vertuous service,
So meritorious, Ferdinand, as yours,
(Yet bashful still, and silent?) should extract
A fuller price then impudence exact:
And this is now the wages it must have;
My daughter is thy wife, my wealth thy slave.

FERDINAND

Good Madam pinch; I sleep: does my Lord mock,
And you assist? Custom's inverted quite;
For old men now adays do flout the young.

BENVOGLIO

Fetch Violanta. As I intend this
Religiously, let my soul finde joy or pain.

[Exit **ANGELINA**.

FERDINAND

My honor'd Lord and Master, if I hold
That worth could merit such felicitie,
You bred it in me, and first purchas'd it;
It is your own: and what productions
In all my faculties my soul begets,
Your very mark is on: you need not add
Rewards to him, that is in debt to you:
You sav'd my life, Sir, in the Massacre;
There you begot me new, since foster'd me.
O! can I serve too much, or pray for you?
Alas, 'tis slender paiment to your bountie.
Your daughter is a paradice, and I
Unworthie to be set there; you may chuse
The royalst seeds of Milain.

BENVOGLIO

Prethee peace,
Thy goodness makes me weep; I am resolv'd:
I am no Lord o' th' time, to tie my blood
To sordid muck; I have enough: my name,
My state and honors I will store in thee,
Whose wisdom will rule well, keep and increase:
A knave or fool, that could confer the like,
Would bate each hour, diminish every day.
Thou art her price-lot then, drawn out by fate;
An honest wise man is a Princes mate.

FERDINAND

Sir, Heaven and you have over-charg'd my brest
With grace beyond my continence; I shall burst:
The blessing you have given me (witness Saints)
I would not change for Millain. But, my Lord,
Is she prepar'd?

BENVOGLIO

What needs Preparative,
Where such a Cordial is prescrib'd as thou?
Thy person and thy virtues in one scale,
Shall poize hers, with her beautie and her wealth;
If not, I add my will unto thy weight;
Thy mother's with her now. Son, take my keys,
And let this preparation for this Marriage,
(This welcome Marriage) long determin'd here,
Be quick, and gorgeous.—Gerrard.

[Enter **GERRARD**.

GERRARD
My good Lord,
My Lord, your brother craves your conference
Instantly, on affairs of high import.

BENVOGLIO
Why, what news?

GERRARD
The Tyrant, my good Lord,
Is sick to death of his old Apoplexie,
Whereon the States advise, that Letters-missive
Be straight dispatcht to all the neighbour-Countreys,
And Schedules too divulg'd on every post,
To enquire the lost Duke forth: their purpose is
To re-instate him.

BENVOGLIO
'Tis a pious deed.
Ferdinand, to my daughter: this delay
(Though to so good a purpose) angers me;
But I'll recover it. Be secret, son.
Go woo with truth and expedition.

[Exit.

FERDINAND
O my unsounded joy! how fares my Gerrard,
My noble twin-friend? fie, thy look is heavie,
Sullen, and sowre; blanch it: didst thou know
My cause of joy, thou 'ldst never sorrow more,
I know thou lov'st me so, How dost thou?

GERRARD
Well,
Too well: my fraught of health my sickness is;

In life, I am dead; by living dying still.

FERDINAND
What sublunary mischief can predominate
A wise man thus? or doth thy frIendship play
(In this antipathous extreme) with mine,
Lest gladness suffocate me? I, I, I do feel
My spirit's turn'd to fire, my blood to air,
And I am like a purifi'd essence
Tri'd from all drossie parts.

GERRARD
Were 't but my life,
The loss were sacrific'd; but virtue
Must for me be slain, and innocence made dust.

FERDINAND
Fare well good Gerrard.

GERRARD
Dearest friend, stay.

FERDINAND
Sad thoughts are no companions for me now,
Much less sad words: thy bosom bindes some secret,
Which do not trust me with; for mine retains
Another, which I must conceal from thee.

GERRARD
I would reveal it: 't is a heavie tale:
Canst thou be true, and secret still?

FERDINAND
Why, friend?
If you continue true unto your self,
I have no means of falshood. Lock this door;
Come, yet your prisoner's sure.

GERRARD
Stay, Ferdinand.

FERDINAND
What is this trouble? Love?
Why, thou art capable of any woman.
Doth want oppress thee? I will lighten thee:
Hast thou offended law? My Lord and thine,
And I, will save thy life. Does servitude
Upbraid thy freedom, that she suffers it?

Have patience but three days, and I will make thee
Thy Lords companion. Can a friend do more?

GERRARD
Lend me the means. How can this be?

FERDINAND
First let this Cabinet keep your pawn, and I will trust:
Yet for the form of satisfaction,
Take this my Oath to boot. By my presum'd
Gentrie, and sacred known Christianitie,
I'll die, ere I reveal thy trust.

GERRARD
Then hear it.
Your Lords fair daughter Violanta is
My betrothed wife, goes great with childe by me;
And by this deed both made a prey to Law.
How may I save her life? advise me, friend.

FERDINAND
What did he say? Gerrard, whose voice was that?
O death unto my heart, bane to my soul!
My wealth is vanish'd like the rich mans store:
In one poor minute all my daintie fare
But jugling dishes; my fat hope, despair.

GERRARD
Is this so odious? where's your mirth?

FERDINAND
Why thou
Hast robb'd me of it. Gerrard, draw thy sword;
And if thou lov'st my Mistris chastitie,
Defend it, else I'll cut it from thy heart,
Thy theevish heart that stole it, and restore 't,
Do miracles to gain her.

GERRARD
Was she thine?

FERDINAND
Never, but in my wish, and her fathers vow,
Which now he left with me, on such sure terms;
He call'd me son, and will'd me to provide
My Wedding-preparation.

GERRARD

Strange.

FERDINAND
Come, let's
Kill one another quickly.

GERRARD
Ferdinand, my love is old to her, thine new begot:
I have not wrong'd thee; think upon thine Oath.

FERDINAND
It manacles me, Gerrard, else this hand
Should bear thee to the Law. Fare well for ever:
Since friendship is so fatal, never more
Will I have friend: thou hast put so sure a plea,
That all my weal's litigious made by thee.

GERRARD
I did no crime to you. His love transports him;
And yet I mourn, that cruel destinie
Should make us two thus one anothers cross:
We have lov'd since boys; for the same time cast him
On Lord Benvoglio, that my Aunt and I
Were succour'd by Randulpho: men have call'd us
The parallels of Millain; and some said
We were not much unlike. O Heaven divert,
That we should (ever since that time) be breeding
Mutual destruction.

[Enter **DOROTHEA**.

DOROTHEA
O where are you? you have made a fair hand. By Heaven yonder is your Aunt with my Lady; she came in, just as she was wooing your Mistris for another; and what did me she, but out with her purse, and shew'd all the naked truth, ifaith. Fie upon you, you should never trust an old woman with a secret; they cannot hold; they cannot hold so well as we, and you'ld hang 'em. First, there was swearing and staring, then there was howling and weeping, and O my daughter, and O my mother.

GERRARD
The effect, the effect.

DOROTHEA
Marry no way, but one with you.

GERRARD
Why welcom. Shall she scape?

DOROTHEA

Nay, she has made her scape already.

GERRARD
Why, is she gone?

DOROTHEA
The scape of her virginitie, I mean.
You men are as dull, you can conceive nothing;
You think it is enough to beget.

GERRARD
I; but surely, Dorothea, that scap'd not;
Her maiden-head suffer'd.

DOROTHEA
And you were the Executioner.

GERRARD
But what's the event? lord, how thou starv'st me, Doll!

DOROTHEA
Lord how thou starv'st me, Doll? By Heaven I would fain see you cry a little. Do you stand now, as if you could get a child? Come, I'll rack you no more: This is the heart of the business: always provided, Signior, that if it please the fates to make you a Lord, you be not proud, nor forget your poor handmaid Doll, who was partly accessary to the incision of this Holofernian Maidenhead.

GERRARD
I will forget my name first. Speak.

DOROTHEA
Then thus; My Lady knows all; her sorrow is reasonably well digested; has vow'd to conceal it from my Lord, till delay ripen things better; Wills you to attend her this evening at the back gate; I'll let you in; where her own Confessor shall put you together lawfully, e'r the child be born; which birth is very near, I can assure you: all your charge is your vigilance; and to bring with you some trusty Nurse, to convey the Infant out of the house.

GERRARD
Oh beam of comfort, take! go, tell my Lady
I pray for her as I walk: my joys so flow,
That what I speak or do, I do not know.

[Exeunt.

SCENE III

Another Room in the Same

[Dumb Shew.

[Enter **VIOLANTA** at one door, weeping, supported by **CORNELIA** and a **FRIAR**; at another door, Angelina weeping, attended by **DOROTHEA**. **VIOLANTA** kneels down for pardon. **ANGELINA** shewing remorse, takes her up, and cheers her; so doth **CORNELIA**. **ANGELINA** sends **DOROTHEA** for **GERRARD**. Enter **GERRARD** with **DOROTHEA**: **ANGELINA** and **CORNELIA** seem to chide him, shewing **VIOLANTA'S** heavy plight: **VIOLANTA** rejoyceth in him: he makes signes of sorrow, intreating pardon: **ANGELINA** brings **GERRARD** and **VIOLANTA** to the **FRIAR**; he joyns them hand in hand, takes a Ring from **GERRARD**, puts it on **VIOLANTA'S** finger; blesseth them; **GERRARD** kisseth her: the **FRIAR** takes his leave. **VIOLANTA** makes shew of great pain, is instantly conveyed in by the **WOMEN**, **GERRARD** is bid stay; he walks in meditation, seeming to pray. Enter **DOROTHEA**, whispers him, sends him out. Enter **GERRARD** with a **NURSE** blindfold; gives her a purse. To them Enter **ANGELINA** and **CORNELIA** with an **INFANT**; they present it to **GERRARD**; he kisseth and blesseth it; puts it into the **NURSES** arms, kneels, and takes his leave. Exeunt **ALL** severally.

SCENE IV

Another Room with a Curtain in the Background

[Enter **BENVOGLIO** and **RANDULPHO**.

BENVOGLIO
He's dead, you say then.

RANDULPHO
Certainly: and to hear
The people now dissect him now he's gone,
Makes my ears burn, that lov'd him not: such Libels,
Such Elegies and Epigrams they have made,
More odious than he was. Brother, great men
Had need to live by love, meting their deeds
With virtues rule; sound, with the weight of judgement,
Their privat'st action: for though while they live
Their power and policie masque their villanies,
Their bribes, their lust, pride, and ambition,
And make a many slaves to worship 'em,
That are their flatterers, and their bawds in these:
These very slaves shall, when these great beasts dye,
Publish their bowels to the vulgar eye.

BENVOGLIO
'Fore Heaven 'tis true. But is Rinaldo (brother) our good
Duke, heard of living?

RANDULPHO

Living, Sir, and will be shortly with the Senate: has
Been close conceal'd at Mantua, and reliev'd:
But what's become of his? no tidings yet?
But brother, till our good Duke shall arrive,
Carry this news, here. Where's your Ferdinand?

BENVOGLIO
Oh busie, Sir, about this marriage:
And yet my Girl o'th' suddain is fall'n sick:
You'll see her e'r you go?

RANDULPHO
Yes; well I love her;
And yet I wish I had another daughter
To gratifie my Gerrard, who by Heaven
Is all the glory of my family,
But has too much worth to live so obscure;
I'll have him Secretary of Estate
Upon the Dukes return: for credit me,
The value of that Gentleman's not known;
His strong abilities are fit to guide
The whole Republique: he hath Learning, youth,
Valour, discretion, honesty of a Saint;
His Aunt is wondrous good too.

BENVOGLIO
You have spoke
The very character of Ferdinand:
One is the others mirror.

[The curtain is drawn, **VIOLANTA** is discovered in a bed; **ANGELINA** and **DOROTHEA** sitting by her.

How now, Daughter?

RANDULPHO
How fares my Neece?

VIOLANTA
A little better, Uncle, then I was,
I thank you.

RANDULPHO
Brother, a meer cold.

ANGELINA
It was a cold and heat, I think: but Heaven be thanked
We have broken that away.

BENVOGLIO
And yet, Violanta,
You'll lie alone still, and you see what's got.

DOROTHEA
Sure, Sir, when this was got, she had a bed-fellow.

RANDULPHO
What has her chollick left her in her belly?

DOROTHEA
'T has left her, but she has had a sore fit.

RANDULPHO
I, that same Collick and Stone's inherent to us
O' th' womans side: our Mothers had them both.

DOROTHEA
So has she had, Sir. How these old fornicators talk! she had more
Need of Mace-Ale, and Rhenish-wine Caudles, heaven knows,
Then your aged Discipline.

BENVOGLIO
Say?

[Enter **FERDINAND** in mourning.

ANGELINA
She will have the man; and on recovery
Will wholly be dispos'd by you.

BENVOGLIO
That's my wench:
How now? what change is this? why Ferdinand,
Are these your Robes of joy should be indu'd?
Doth Hymen wear black? I did send for you
To have my honorable Brother witness
The Contract I will make 'twixt you and her.
Put off all doubt; she loves ye? what d' ye say?

RANDULPHO
Speak man, Why look you so distractedly?

FERDINAND
There are your keys, Sir: I'll no Contracts, I
Divinest Violanta, I will serve you
Thus on my knees, and pray for you: Juno, Lucina fer opem.
My inequality ascends no higher:

I dare not marry you.

BENVOGLIO
How's this?

FERDINAND
Good night,
I have a friend has almost made me mad:
I weep sometimes, and instantly can laugh:
Nay, I do dance, and sing, and suddenly
Roar like a storm. Strange tricks these, are they not?
And wherefore all this? Shall I tell you? no,
Thorow mine ears, my heart a plague hath caught,
And I have vow'd to keep it close, not shew
My grief to any; for it has no cure.
On, wandring steps, to some remote place move:
I'll keep my vow, though I have lost my Love.

[Exit.

BENVOGLIO
'Fore heaven, distracted for her! fare you well:
I'll watch his steps; for I no joy shall find,
Till I have found his cause, and calm'd his mind.

[Exit.

RANDULPHO
He's overcome with joy.

ANGELINA
'Tis very strange.

RANDULPHO
Well, Sister, I must leave you; the time's busie.
Violanta, chear you up; and I pray Heaven
Restore each to their love, and health again.

[Exit.

VIOLANTA
Amen, Great Uncle. Mother, what a chance
Unluckily is added to my woe,
In this young Gentleman!

ANGELINA
True, Violanta:
It grieves me much. Doll, go you instantly,

And find out Gerrard; tell him his friends hap,
And let him use best means to comfort him;
But as his life preserve this secret still.

VIOLANTA
Mother, I'ld not offend you: might not Gerrard
Steal in, and see me in the evening?

ANGELINA
Well,
Bid him do so.

VIOLANTA
Heavens blessing o' your heart.
Do ye not call Child-bearing, Travel, Mother?

ANGELINA
Yes.

VIOLANTA
It well may be, The bare-foot traveller
That's born a Prince, and walks his pilgrimage,
Whose tender feet kiss the remorseless stones
Only, ne'er felt a travel like to it.
Alas, dear Mother, you groan'd thus for me,
And yet how disobedient have I been!

ANGELINA
Peace, Violanta, thou hast always been
Gentle and good.

VIOLANTA
Gerrard is better, Mother:
Oh if you knew the implicite innocency
Dwells in his brest, you'ld love him like your Prayers.
I see no reason but my Father might
Be told the truth, being pleas'd for Ferdinand
To wooe himself: and Gerard ever was
His full comparative: my Uncle loves him,
As he loves Ferdinand.

ANGELINA
No, not for the world,
Since his intent is cross'd: lov'd Ferdinand
Thus ruin'd, and a child got out of wedlock:
His madness would pursue ye both to death.

VIOLANTA

As you please (mother:) I am now, methinks,
Even in the land of ease; I'll sleep.

ANGELINA
Draw in
The bed nearer the fire: silken rest,
Tie all thy cares up.

[Exeunt.

SCENE V

A Grove

[Enter **FERDINAND** and **BENVOGLIO** privately after him.

FERDINAND
Oh blessed solitude! here my griefs may speak;
And sorrow, I will argue with thee now:
Nothing will keep me company: the flowers
Die at my moan; the gliding silver streams
Hasten to flee my lamentations;
The air rolls from 'em; and the Golden Sun
Is smother'd pale as Phœbe with my sighs:
Only the earth is kind, that stays. Then earth,
To thee will I complain. Why do the Heavens
Impose upon me Love, what I can ne'er enjoy?
Before fruition was impossible,
I did not thirst it. Gerrard, she is thine,
Seal'd and deliver'd; but 'twas ill to stain
Her virgin state, e'r ye were married.
Poor Infant, what's become of thee? thou know'st not
The woe thy parents brought thee to. Dear earth,
Bury this close in thy sterility;
Be barren to this seed, let it not grow;
For if it do, 'twill bud no Violet
Nor Gillyflower, but wild Brier, or rank Rue,
Unsavory and hurtful.

BENVOGLIO
Ferdinand,
Thy steel hath digg'd the Earth, thy words my Heart.

FERDINAND
Oh! I have violated faith, betraid
My friend and innocency.

BENVOGLIO
Desperate youth,
Violate not thy soul too: I have showers
For thee, young man; but Gerrard flames for thee.
Was thy base pen made to dash out mine honor,
And prostitute my Daughter? Bastard, whore,
Come, turn thy femal tears into revenge,
Which I will quench my thirst with, e'r I see
Daughter, or Wife, or branded Family.
By Heaven both dye: and for amends,
Ferd'nando be my heir. I'll to my brother,
First tell him all, then to the Duke for justice:
This morning he's receiv'd. Mountains nor Seas
Shall bar my flight to vengeance: the foul stain
Printed on me, thy bloud shall rinse again.

[Exit.

FERDINAND
I have transgress'd all goodness, witlesly
Rais'd mine own curses from posterity:
I'll follow, to redress in what I may;
If not, your heir can dye as well as they.

[Exit.

SCENE VI

An Apartment in the Palace

[Dumb Shew.

[Enter **DUKE RINALDO** with **ATTENDANTS**, at one door; **STATES**, **RANDULPHO**, and **GERRARD**, at another: they kneel to the **DUKE**, he accepts their obedience, and raises them up: they prefer **GERRARD** to the **DUKE**, who entertains him: they seat the **DUKE** in State. Enter **BENVOGLIO** and **FERDINAND**: **BENVOGLIO** kneels for justice; **FERDINAND** seems to restrein him. **BENVOGLIO** gives the **DUKE** a paper; **DUKE** reads, frowns on **GERRARD**. shews the paper to the **STATES**, they seem sorry, consult, cause the **GUARD** to apprehend him; they go off with him. Then **RANDULPHO** and **BENVOGLIO** seem to crave justice; **DUKE** vows it, and exit with his **ATTENDANTS**. **RANDULPHO, BENVOGLIO** and **FERDINAND** confer.

[Enter to them **CORNELIA** with **TWO SERVANTS**; she seems to expostulate, **RANDULPHO** in scorn, causeth her to be thrust out poorly. Exit **RANDULPHO**. **BENVOGLIO** beckons **FERDINAND** to him (with much seeming passion) swears him; then stamps with his foot. Enter **DOROTHEA** with a Cup, weeping, she delivers it to **FERDINAND** who with discontent exit; and exeunt **BENVOGLIO** and **DOROTHEA**.

A Room in Benvoglio's House

[Enter **VIOLANTA**.

VIOLANTA
Gerrard not come? nor Dorothy return'd?
What averse star rul'd my Nativity?
The time to night has been as dilatory
As languishing Consumptions. But till now
I never durst say, my Gerrard was unkind.
Heaven grant all things go well; and nothing does,
If he be ill, which I much fear: my dreams
Have been portentous. I did think I saw
My Love araid for battel with a beast,
A hideous Monster, arm'd with teeth and claws,
Grinning, and venemous, that sought to make
Both us a prey: on's tail was lash'd in bloud
Law: and his forehead I did plainly see
Held Characters that spell'd Authority.
This rent my slumbers; and my fearful soul
Ran searching up and down my dismaid breast,
To find a Port t'escape. Good faith, I am cold;
But Gerrard's love is colder: here I'll sit,
And think my self away.

[Enter **FERDINAND** with a Cup and a Letter.

FERDINAND
The peace of Love
Attend the sweet Violanta: Read,
For the sad news I bring, I do not know;
Only I am sworn to give you that, and this.

VIOLANTA
Is it from Gerrard? gentle Ferdinand,
How glad am I to see you thus well restor'd!
In troth he never wrong'd you in his life,
Nor I, but always held fair thoughts of you,
Knew not my Fathers meaning, till of late;
Could never have known it soon enough: for Sir,
Gerrard's, and my affection began
In infancy: My Uncle brought him oft
In long coats hither; you were such another;

The little boy would kiss me, being a child,
And say, he lov'd me; give me all his toys,
Bracelets, Rings, Sweet-meats, all his Rosie-smiles:
I then would stand, and stare upon his eyes,
Play with his locks, and swear I lov'd him too;
For sure, methought, he was a little Love,
He woo'd so prettily in innocence,
That then he warm'd my fancy; for I felt
A glimmering beam of Love kindle my bloud,
Both which, time since hath made a flame and floud.

FERDINAND
Oh gentle innocent! methinks it talks
Like a child still, whose white simplicity
Never arriv'd at sin. Forgive me, Lady,
I have destroy'd Gerrard, and thee; rebell'd
Against Heavens Ordinance; dis-pair'd two Doves,
Made 'em sit mourning; slaughter'd Love, and cleft
The heart of all integrity. This breast
Was trusted with the secret of your vow
By Gerrard, and reveal'd it to your Father.

VIOLANTA
Hah!

FERDINAND
Read, and curse me.

VIOLANTA
Neither: I will never
Nor Write, nor Read again.

FERDINAND
My pennance be it.
Reads. Your Labyrinth is found, your Lust proclaim'd.

VIOLANTA
Lust? Humh:
My Mother sure felt none, when I was got.

FERDINAND
I and the Law implacably offended.
Gerrard's imprison'd, and to dye.

VIOLANTA
Oh Heaven!

FERDINAND

And you to suffer with reproach and scoffs
A publick execution; I have sent you
An Antidote 'gainst shame, poison; by him
You have most wrong'd: give him your penitent tears.

VIOLANTA

Humh: 'tis not truth.

FERDINAND

Drink, and farewel for ever:
And though thy whoredom blemish thy whole line,
Prevent the Hangmans stroke, and die like mine.

VIOLANTA

Oh woe is me for Gerrard: I have brought
Confusion on the noblest Gentleman
That ever truly lov'd. But we shall meet
Where our condemners shall not, and enjoy
A more refin'd affection than here;
No Law, nor Father hinders marriage there
'Twixt souls Divinely affi'd, as (sure) ours were:
There we will multiply, and generate joyes
Like fruitful Parents. Luckless Ferdinand,
Where's the good old Gentlewoman, my Husbands Aunt?

FERDINAND

Thrust from you Uncle to all poverty.

VIOLANTA

Alas the pity: reach me, Sir, the cup;
I'll say my prayers, and take my Fathers Physick.

FERDINAND

Oh villain that I was, I had forgot
To spill the rest, and am unable now
To stir to hinder her.

VIOLANTA

What ail you, Sir?

FERDINAND

Your Father is a monster, I a villain,
This tongue has kill'd you, pardon, Violanta,
Oh pardon, Gerrard; and for sacrifice,
Accept my life, to expiate my fault.
I have drunk up the poison.

VIOLANTA

Thou art not so
Uncharitable: a better fellow far,
Thou'st left me halfe. Sure death is now a-dry,
And calls for more bloud still to quench his thirst.
I pledge thee Ferdinand, to Gerrards health:
Dear Gerrard, poor Aunt, and unfortunate friend,
Ay me, that Love should breed true Lovers end.

FERDINAND
Stay Madam, stay; help hoa, for Heavens sake help;
Improvident man, that good I did intend
For satisfaction, saving of her life,
My equal cruel Stars made me forget.

[Enter **ANGELINA** with **TWO SERVANTS**.

ANGELINA
What spectacle of death assaults me? oh!

VIOLANTA
My dearest Mother, I am dead, I leave
Father, and friends, and life, to follow Love.
Good Mother, love my Child, that did no ill.
Fie, how men lie, that say, death is a pain:
Or has he chang'd his nature? like soft sleep
He seizes me. Your blessing. Last, I crave,
That I may rest by Gerrard in his grave.

FERDINAND
There lay me too: oh! noble Mistriss, I
Have caus'd all this; and therefore justly dye.
That key will open all.

ANGELINA
Oh viperous Father!
For Heavens sake, bear 'em in: run for Physitians,
And Medicines quickly: Heaven, thou shalt not have her
Yet; 'tis too soon: Alas, I have no more,
And taking her away, thou rob'st the poor.

[Exeunt.

SCENE VIII

An Open Place in the City

[Flourish.

[Enter **DUKE**, **STATES**, **RANDULPHO**, **BENVOGLIO**, **GERRARD**, **EXECUTIONER**, **GUARD**.

DUKE
The Law, as greedy as your red desire
Benvoglio, hath cast this man: 'Tis pity
So many excellent parts are swallow'd up
In one foul wave. Is Violanta sent for?
Our Justice must not lop a branch, and let
The body grow still.

BENVOGLIO
Sir, she will be here
Alive or dead, I am sure.

GERRARD
How chearfully my countenance comments death!
That which makes men seem horrid, I will wear
Like to an Ornament. Oh Violanta!
Might my life only satisfie the Law,
How jocundly my soul would enter Heaven!
Why shouldst thou dye? thou wither'st in thy bud,
As I have seen a Rose, e'er it was blown.
I do beseech your Grace, the Statute may
(In this case made) be read: not that I hope
T'extenuate my offence or penalty,
But to see whether it lay hold on her.
And since my death is more exemplary
Than just, this publick Reading will advise
Caution to others.

DUKE
Read it.

RANDULPHO
Brother, does not
Your soul groan under this severity?

[Statute read.

"A Statute provided in case of unequal Matches, Marriages against Parents consent, stealing of Heirs, Rapes, Prostitutions, and such like: That if any person meanly descended, or ignorant of his own Parentage, which implies as much, shall with a foul intent, unlawfully sollicite the Daughter of any Peer of the Dukedom, he shall for the same offence forfeit his right hand: but if he further prostitute her to his Lust, he shall first have his right hand cut off, and then suffer death by the common Executioner. After whom, the Lady so offending, shall likewise the next day, in the same manner, dye for the Fact."

GERRARD
This Statute has more cruelty than sense:
I see no ray of Mercy. Must the Lady
Suffer death too? suppose she were inforc'd,
By some confederates born away, and ravish'd;
Is she not guiltless?

DUKE
Yes, if it be prov'd.

GERRARD
This case is so: I ravish'd Violanta.

STATE
Who ever knew a Rape produce a child?

BENVOGLIO
Pish, these are idle. Will your grace command
The Executioner proceed?

DUKE
Your Office.

GERRARD
Farewell to thy inticing vanity,
Thou round gilt box, that dost deceive man's eye:
The wise man knows, when open thou art broke,
The treasure thou includ'st, is dust and smoke,
Even thus, I cast thee by. My Lords, the Law
Is but the great mans mule, he rides on it,
And tramples poorer men under his feet;
Yet when they come to knock at yon bright Gate,
Ones Rags shall enter, 'fore the others State.
Peace to ye all: here, sirrah, strike: this hand
Hath Violanta kiss'd a thousand times;
It smells sweet ever since: this was the hand
Plighted my faith to her: do not think thou canst
Cut that in sunder with my hand. My Lord,
As free from speck as this arm is, my heart
Is of foul Lust, and every vein glides here
As full of truth. Why does thy hand shake so?
'Tis mine must be cut off, and that is firm;
For it was ever constant.

[Enter **CORNELIA**, veiled.

CORNELIA
Hold; your Sentence

Unjustly is pronounced, my Lord: this blow
Cuts your hand off; for his is none of yours:
But Violanta's given in Holy marriage
Before she was delivered, consummated
With the free Will of her Mother, by her Confessor,
In Lord Benvoglio's house.

GERRARD
Alas good Aunt,
That helps us nothing; else I had reveal'd it.

DUKE
What woman's this?

BENVOGLIO
A base confederate
In this proceeding, kept of alms long time
By him; who now expos'd to misery,
Talks thus distractedly. Attach her, Guard.

RANDULPHO
Your cruelty brother will have end.

CORNELIA
You'd best
Let them attach my tongue.

DUKE
Good woman, peace:
For were this truth, it doth not help thy Nephew;
The Law's infring'd by their disparity,
That forfeits both their lives.

CORNELIA
Sir, with your pardon,
Had your Grace ever children?

DUKE
Thou hast put
A question, whose sharp point toucheth my heart:
I had two little Sons, twins, who were both
(With my good Dutchess) slain, as I did hear;
At that time when my Dukedom was surpriz'd.

CORNELIA
I have heard many say my gracious Lord
That I was wondrous like her.

ALL
Ha?

DUKE
By all mans joy, it is Cornelia,
My dearest wife.

CORNELIA
To ratifie me her,
Come down, Alphonso, one of those two twins,
And take thy Fathers blessing: thou hast broke
No Law, thy birth being above thy wives:
Ascanio is the other, nam'd Fernando,
Who by remote means, to my Lord Benvoglio
I got preferr'd; and in poor habits clad,
(You fled, and th' innovation laid again)
I wrought my self into Randulpho's service,
With my eldest boy; yet never durst reveal
What they and I were, no, not to themselves,
Until the Tyrants death.

DUKE
My joy has fill'd me
Like a full-winded sail: I cannot speak.

GERRARD
Fetch Violanta and my brother.

BENVOGLIO
Run,
Run like a spout, you rogue: a pox o' poison,
That little whore I trusted, will betray me.
Stay, hangman, I have work for you; there's Gold;
Cut off my head, or hang me presently.

[Soft Musick.

[Enter **ANGELINA** with the bodies of **FERDINAND** and **VIOLANTA** on a bier; **DOROTHEA** carrying the Cup
and Letter, which she gives to the **DUKE**: he reads, seems sorrowful; shews it to **CORNELIA** and
GERRARD: they lament over the bier. **RANDULPHO** and **BENVOGLIO** seem fearful, and seem to report to
ANGELINA and **DOROTHEA**, what hath passed before.

RANDULPHO
This is your rashness, brother.

DUKE
Oh joy, thou wert too great to last;
This was a cruel turning to our hopes,

Unnatural Father: poor Ascanio.

GERRARD
Oh mother! let me be Gerrard again,
And follow Violanta.

CORNELIA
Oh my Son—

DUKE
Your lives yet, bloudy men shall answer this.

DOROTHEA
I must not see 'em longer grieve. My Lord,
Be comforted; let sadness generally
Forsake each eye and bosom; they both live:
For poison, I infus'd meer Opium;
Holding compulsive perjury less sin
Than such a loathed murther would have bin.

ALL
Oh blessed Maiden.

DOROTHEA
Musick, gently creep
Into their ears, and fright hence lazy sleep.

[Music.

Morpheus, command thy servant sleep
In leaden chains no longer keep
This Prince and Lady: Rise, wake, rise,
And round about convey your eyes:
Rise Prince, go greet thy Father and thy Mother;
Rise thou, t'imbrace thy Husband and thy Brother.

DUKE & CORNELIUS
Son, Daughter.

FERDINAND
Father, Mother, Brother.

GERRARD
Wife.

VIOLANTA
Are we not all in Heaven?

GERRARD
Faith, very near it.

FERDINAND
How can this be?

DUKE
Hear it.

DOROTHEA
If I had serv'd you right, I should have seen
Your old pate off, e'r I had reveald.

BENVOGLIO
Oh wench!
Oh honest wench! if my wife die, I'll marry thee:
There's my reward.

FERDINAND
'Tis true.

DUKE
'Tis very strange.

GERRARD
Why kneel you honest Master?

FERDINAND
My good Lord.

GERRARD
Dear Mother.

DUKE
Rise, rise, all are friends: I owe ye
for all their boards: And wench, take thou the man
Whose life thou sav'dst; less cannot pay the merit.
How shall I part my kiss? I cannot: Let
One generally therefore joyn our cheeks.
A pen of Iron, and a leaf of Brass,
To keep this Story to Eternity:
And a Promethean Wit. Oh sacred Love,
Nor chance, nor death can thy firm truth remove.

[Exeunt.

KING
Now Isabella.

[Flourish.

ISABELLA
This can true Love do.
I joy they all so happily are pleas'd:
The Ladies and the Brothers must triumph.

KING
They do:
For Cupid scorns but t' have his triumph too.

THE TRIUMPH OF DEATH

SCENE I

Angers. A Room in the House of L'avall

[Flourish.

[Enter divers **MUSICIANS**, then certain **SINGERS** bearing Bannerets inscribed, **TRUTH**, **LOYALTY**, **PATIENCE**, **CONCORD**: Next **GERRARD** and **FERDINAND** with Garlands of Roses: Then **VIOLANTA**, Last, a Chariot drawn by **TWO CUPIDS**, and a **CUPID** sitting in it.

[Flourish.

[Enter **PROLOGUE**.

Love, and the strength of fair affection
(Most royal Sir) what long seem'd lost, have won
Their perfect ends, and crown'd those constant hearts
With lasting Triumph, whose most virtuous parts,
Worthy desires, and love, shall never end.
Now turn we round the Scæne, and (Great Sir) lend
A sad and serious eye to this of Death,
This black and dismal Triumph; where man's breath,
Desert, and guilty bloud ascend the Stage,
And view the Tyrant, ruind in his rage.

[Exit.

[Flourish.

[Enter **L'AVALL**, **GABRIELLA** and **MARIA**.

GABRIELLA

No, good my Lord, I am not now to find
Your long neglect of me; All those affections
You came first clad in to my love, like Summer,
Lusty and full of life: all those desires
That like the painted Spring bloom'd round about ye,
Giving the happy promise of an Harvest,
How have I seen drop off, and fall forgotten!
With the least lustre of anothers beauty,
How oft (forgetful Lord) have I been blasted!
Was I so eas'ly won? or did this body
Yield to your false embraces with less labour
Then if you had carried some strong Town?

L'AVALL

Good Gabriella.

GABRIELLA

Could all your subtilties and sighs betray me.
The vows ye shook me with, the tears ye drown'd me,
Till I came fairly off with honor'd Marriage?
Oh fie, my Lord.

L'AVALL

Prethee good Gabriella.

GABRIELLA

Would I had never known ye, nor your honors,
They are stuck too full of griefs: oh happy women,
That plant your Love in equal honest bosoms,
Whose sweet desires like Roses set together,
Make one another happy in their blushes,
Growing and dying without sense of greatness,
To which I am a slave! and that blest Sacrament
That daily makes millions of happy mothers, link'd me
To this man's Lust alone, there left me.
I dare not say I am his wife, 'tis dangerous:
His Love, I cannot say: alas, how many?

L'AVALL

You grow too warm; pray ye be content, you best know,
The times necessity, and how our marriage
Being so much unequal to mine honor,
While the Duke lives, I standing high in favour;
And whilst I keep that safe, next to the Dukedom,
Must not be known, without my utter ruine.
Have patience for a while, and do but dream wench,
The glory of a Dutchess. How she tires me!

How dull and leaden is my appetite
To that stale beauty now! oh, I could curse
And crucifie my self for childish doating
Upon a face that feeds not with fresh Figures
Every fresh hour: she is now a surfet to me.

[Enter **GENTILLE**.

Who's that? Gentille? I charge ye, no acquaintance
You nor your Maid with him, nor no discourse
Till times are riper.

GENTILLE
Fie, my Noble Lord,
Can you be now a stranger to the Court,
When your most virtuous Bride, the beauteous Hellena
Stands ready like a Star to gild your happiness,
When Hymens lusty fires are now a lighting,
And all the Flower of Anjou?

L'AVALL
Some few trifles,
For matter of adornment, have a little
Made me so slow, Gentille, which now in readiness,
I am for Court immediately.

GENTILLE
Take heed, Sir,
This is no time for trifling, nor she no Lady
To be now entertain'd with toys: 'twill cost ye—

L'AVALL
Y'are an old Cock, Gentille.

GENTILLE
By your Lordships favour.

L'AVALL
Prethee away; 'twill lose time.

GENTILLE
Oh my Lord,
Pardon me that by all means.

L'AVALL
We have business
A-foot man, of more moment.

GENTILLE
Then my manners?
I know none, nor I seek none.

L'AVALL
Take to morrow.

GENTILLE
Even now, by your Lordships leave. Excellent Beauty.
My service here I ever dedicate,
In honor of my best friend, your dead Father,
To you his living virtue, and wish heartily,
That firm affection that made us two happy,
May take as deep undying root, and flourish
Betwixt my Daughter Casta, and your goodness,
Who shall be still your servant.

GABRIELLA
I much thank ye.

L'AVALL
Pox o' this dreaming puppy. Will ye go, Sir?

GENTILLE
A little more, Good Lord.

L'AVALL
Not now, by Heaven
Come, I must use ye.

GENTILLE
Goodness dwell still with you.

[Exeunt **GENTILLE** and **L'AVALL**.

GABRIELLA
The sight of this old Gentleman, Maria,
Pulls to my mine eyes again the living Picture
Of Perolot his virtuous Son, my first Love,
That dy'd at Orleance.

MARIA
You have felt both fortunes,
And in extreams, poor Lady; for young Perolot,
Being every way unable to maintain you,
Durst not make known his love to Friend or Father:
My Lord Lavall, being powerful, and you poor,
Will not acknowledge you.

GABRIELLA
No more: Let's in wench:
There let my Lute speak my Laments, they have tired me.

[Exeunt.

SCENE II

Before the Palace

[Enter **TWO COURTIERS**.

1ST COURTIER
I grant, the Duke is wondrous provident
In his now planting for succession,
I know his care as honourable in the choice too.
Marines fair virtuous daughter; but what's all this?
To what end excellent arrives this travel,
When he that bears the main roof is so rotten?

2ND COURTIER
You have hit it now indeed: For if Fame lye not
He is untemperate.

1ST COURTIER
You express him poorly,
Too gentle Sir: the most deboist and barbarous;
Believe it, the most void of all humanity,
Howe'r his cunning, cloak it to his Uncle,
And those his pride depends upon.

2ND COURTIER
I have heard too,
Given excessively to drink.

1ST COURTIER
Most certain,
And in that drink most dangerous: I speak these things
To one I know loves truth, and dares not wrong her.

2ND COURTIER
You may speak on.

1ST COURTIER
Uncertain as the Sea, Sir,

Proud and deceitful as his sins Great Master;
His appetite to Women (for there he carries
His main Sail spread) so boundles, and abominably,
That but to have her name by that tongue spoken,
Poisons the virtue of the purest Virgin.

2ⁿᵈ COURTIER

I am sorry for young Gabriella then,
A Maid reputed, ever of fair carriage,
For he has been noted visiting.

1ˢᵗ COURTIER

She is gone then,
Or any else, that promises, or power,
Gifts, or his guilful vows can work upon,
But these are but poor parcels.

2ⁿᵈ COURTIER

'Tis great pity.

1ˢᵗ COURTIER

Nor want these sins a chief Saint to befriend 'em,
The Devil follows him; and for a truth, Sir,
Appears in visible figure often to him,
At which time he's possest with sudden trances,
Cold deadly sweats, and griping of the conscience,
Tormented strangely, as they say.

2ⁿᵈ COURTIER

Heaven turn him:
This marriage-day mayst thou well curse, fair Hellen.
But let's go view the ceremony.

1ˢᵗ COURTIER

I'll walk with you.

[Exeunt.

SCENE III

A Street Before L'Avall's House

[Musick.

[Enter **GABRIELLA**, and **MARIA** above. And **L'AVALL**, **BRIDE**, **STATES** in solemnity as to marriage; and pass over; viz. **DUKE**, **MARINE**, **LONGAVILLE**.

MARIA

I hear 'em come.

GABRIELLA

Would I might never hear more.

MARIA

I told you still: but you were so incredulous.
See, there they kiss.

GABRIELLA

Adders be your embraces.
The poison of a rotten heart, oh Hellen!
Blast thee as I have been; just such a flattery,
With that same cunning face, that smile upon't,
Oh mark it Marie, mark it seriously,
That Master smile caught me.

MARIA

There's the old Duke, and
Marine her Father.

GABRIELLA

Oh!

MARIA

There Longaville—
The Ladies now.

GABRIELLA

Oh, I am murder'd, Marie.
Beast, most inconstant beast.

MARIA

There.

GABRIELLA

There I am not;
No more I am not there: Hear me, oh Heaven!
And all you powers of Justice bow down to me;
But you of pity dye. I am abus'd,
She that depended on your Providence,
She is abus'd: your honor is abus'd.
That noble piece ye made, and call'd it man,
Is turn'd to Devil: all the world's abus'd:
Give me a womans Will, provok'd to mischief,
A two-edg'd heart; my suffering thoughts to wild-fires,

And my embraces to a timeless grave turn.

MARIA
Here I'll step in, for 'tis an act of merit.

GABRIELLA
I am too big to utter more.

MARIA
Take time then.

[Exeunt.

[Enter **GENTILLE** and **CASTA**.

GENTILLE
This solitary life at home undoes thee,
Obscures thy beauty first, which should prefer thee;
Next fills thee full of sad thoughts, which thy years
Must not arrive at yet, they choak thy sweetness;
Follow the time, my Girl, and it will bring thee
Even to the fellowship of the noblest women,
Hellen her self, to whom I would prefer thee,
And under whom this poor and private carriage,
Which I am only able yet to reach at,
Being cast off, and all thy sweets at lustre,
Will take thee as a fair friend, and prefer thee.

CASTA
Good Sir, be not so cruel as to seek
To kill that sweet content y'have bred me to:
Have I not here enough to thank Heaven for?
The free air uncorrupted with new flattery.
The water that I touch, unbrib'd with odours
To make me sweet to others: the pure fire
Not smothered up, and choak'd with lustful incense
To make my bloud sweat; but burning clear and high,
Tells me my mind must flame up so to Heaven.
What should I do at Court, wear rich apparel?
Methinks these are as warm: And for your state, Sir,
Wealthy enough; Is it you would have me proud,
And like a Pageant, stuck up for amazements?

Teach not your child to tread that path, for fear (Sir)
Your dry bones after death, groan in your grave
The miseries that follow.

GENTILLE
Excellent Casta.

CASTA
When shall I pray again? (a Courtier)
Or when I do, to what God? what new body
And new face must I make me, with new manners?
For I must be no more my self. Whose Mistriss
Must I be first? with whose sin-offering season'd?
And when I am grown so great and glorious
With prostitution of my burning beauties,
That great Lords kneel, and Princes beg for favours,
Do you think I'll be your Daughter, a poor Gentlemans,
Or know you for my father?

[Enter **L'AVALL**.

GENTILLE
My best Casta.
Oh my most virtuous child! Heaven reigns within thee;
Take thine own choice, sweet child, and live a Saint still.
The Lord Lavall, stand by wench.

L'AVALL
Gabriella,
She cannot, nor she dares not make it known,
My greatness crushes her, when e'er she offers:
Why should I fear her then?

GENTILLE
Come, let's pass on wench.

L'AVALL
Gentille, come hither: who's that Gentlewoman?

GENTILLE
A child of mine, Sir, who observing custome,
Is going to the Monastery to her Prayers.

L'AVALL
A fair one, a most sweet one; fitter far
To beautifie a Court, than make a Votarist.
Go on, fair Beauty, and in your Orizons
Remember me: will ye, fair sweet?

CASTA
Most humbly.

[Exeunt.

L'AVALL
An admirable Beauty: how it fires me!

[Enter a **SPIRIT**.

But she's too full of grace, and I too wicked.
I feel my wonted fit: Defend me, goodness.
Oh! it grows colder still, and stiffer on me,
My hair stands up, my sinews shake and shrink;
Help me good Heaven, and good thoughts dwell within me.
Oh get thee gone, thou evil evil spirit,
Haunt me no more, I charge thee.

SPIRIT
Yes L'avall:
Thou art my vassal, and the slave to mischief,
I blast thee with new sin: pursue thy pleasure;
Casta is rare and sweet, a blowing Beauty;
Set thy desires a fire, and never quench 'em
Till thou enjoy'st her; make her all thy Heaven,
And all thy joy, for she is all true happiness:
Thou art powerful, use command; if that prevail not,
Force her: I'll be thy friend.

L'AVALL
Oh help me, help me.

SPIRIT
Her virtue, like a spell, sinks me to darkness.

[Exit.

[Enter **GENTILLE** and **CASTA**.

GENTILLE
He's here still. How is't, noble Lord? me thinks, Sir,
You look a little wildly. Is it that way?
Is't her you stare on so? I have spy'd your fire, Sir,
But dare not stay the flaming. Come.

L'AVALL
Sweet creature,

Excellent Beauty, do me but the happiness
To be your humblest servant. Oh fair eyes,
Oh blessed, Blessed Sweetness, Divine Virgin!

CASTA
Oh good my Lord, retire into your honor:
You're spoken good and virtuous, plac'd at Helme
To govern others from mischances: from example
Of such fair Chronicles as great ones are,
We do, or sure we should direct our lives.
I know y'are full of worth, a school of virtue
Daily instructing us that live below ye,
I make no doubt, dwells there.

L'AVALL
I cannot answer,
She has struck me dumb with wonder.

CASTA
Goodness guide ye.

[Exeunt.

L'AVALL
She's gone, and with her all light, and has left me
Dark as my black desires. Oh devil lust,
How dost thou hug my bloud, and whisper to me,
There is no day again, no time, no living,
Without this lusty Beauty break upon me!
Let me collect my self, I strive like billows,
Beaten against a rock, and fall a fool still.
I must enjoy her, and I will: from this hour
My thoughts, and all my bus'ness shall be nothing.

[Enter **MARIA**.

My eating, and my sleeping, but her beauty,
And how to work it.

MARIA
Health to my Lord Lavall.
Nay good Sir, do not turn with such displeasure;
I come not to afflict your new born pleasures;
My honour'd Mistriss, neither let that vex ye,
For nothing is intended, but safe to you.

L'AVALL
What of your Mistriss? I am full of bus'ness.

MARIA

I will be short, my Lord; she, loving Lady,
Considering the unequal tie between ye,
And how your ruine with the Duke lay on it,
As also the most noble match now made,
By me sends back all links of marriage,
All Holy Vows, and Rights of Ceremony,
All promises, oaths, tears, and all such pawns
You left in hostage: only her love she cannot,
For that still follows ye, but not to hurt ye;
And still beholds ye Sir, but not to shame ye:
In recompence of which, this is her suit, Sir,
Her poor and last petition, but to grant her,
When weary nights have cloyed ye up with kisses,
(As such must come) the honor of a Mistriss,
The honor but to let her see those eyes,
(Those eyes she doats on, more than gods do goodness)
And but to kiss you only: with this prayer,
(a prayer only to awake your pity)
And on her knees she made it, that this night
You'd bless her with your company at supper.

L'AVALL

I like this well, and now I think on't better,
I'll make a present use from this occasion.

MARIA

Nay, good my Lord, be not so cruel to her
Because she has been yours.

L'AVALL

And to mine own end
A rare way I will work.

MARIA

Can love for ever,
The Love of her (my Lord) so perish in ye?
As ye desire in your desires to prosper.
What gallant under Heaven, but Anjou's Heir then
Can brag so fair a Wife, and sweet a Mistriss?
Good noble Lord.

L'AVALL

Ye mis-apply me, Mary,
Nor do I want true pity to your Lady:
Pity and love tell me, too much I have wrong'd her
To dare to see her more: yet if her sweetness

Can entertain a Mediation,
And it must be a great one that can cure me;
My love again, as far as honor bids me,
My service and my self—

MARIA
That's nobly spoken.

L'AVALL
Shall hourly see her; want shall never know her;
Nor where she has bestow'd her love, repent her.

MARIA
Now whither drives he?

L'AVALL
I have heard Maria,
That no two women in the world more lov'd,
Then thy good Mistriss, and Gentille's fair Daughter.

MARIA
What may this mean? you have heard a truth, my Lord:
But since the secret Love betwixt you two,
My Mistriss durst not entertain such friendship;
Casta is quick, and of a piercing judgement,
And quickly will find out a flaw.

L'AVALL
Hold Marie:
Shrink not, 'tis good gold, wench: prepare a Banquet,
And get that Casta thither; for she's a creature
So full of forcible Divine perswasion,
And so unwearied ever with good office,
And she shall cure my ill cause to my Mistriss,
And make all errors up.

MARIA
I'll doe my best, Sir:
But she's too fearful, coy, and scrupulous,
To leave her Fathers house so late; and bashful
At any mans appearance, that I fear, Sir;
'Twill prove impossible.

L'AVALL
There's more gold, Marie,
And fain thy Mistriss wondrous sick to death, wench.

MARIA

I have ye in the wind now, and I'll pay ye.

L'AVALL
She cannot chuse but come; 'tis charity,
The chief of her profession: undertake this,
And I am there at night; if not, I leave ye.

MARIA
I will not loose this offer, though it fall out
Clean cross to that we cast, I'll undertake it,
I will, my Lord; she shall be there.

L'AVALL
By Heaven?

MARIA
By Heaven she shall.

L'AVALL
Let it be something late then.
For being seen, now force or favour wins her.
My spirits are grown dull, strong wine, and store,
Shall set 'em up again, and make me fit
To draw home at the enterprize I aim at.

[Exit.

MARIA
Go thy waies false Lord, if thou hold'st, thou pay'st
The price of all thy lusts. Thou shalt be there
Thou modest Maid, if I have any working,
And yet thy honor safe; for which this thief
I know has set this meeting: but I'll watch him.

[Enter **PEROLOT**.

PEROLOT
Maria.

MARIA
Are mine eyes mine own? or bless me,
Am I deluded with a flying shadow?

PEROLOT
Why do you start so from me?

MARIA
It speaks sensibly,

And shews a living body: yet I am fearful.

PEROLOT
Give me your hand, good Maria.

MARIA
He feels warm too.

PEROLOT
And next your lips.

MARIA
He kisses perfectly.
Nay, and the Devil be no worse: you are Perolot.

PEROLOT
I was, and sure I should be: Can a small distance,
And ten short moneths take from your memory
The figure of your friend, that you stand wondring?
Be not amaz'd, I am the self-same Perolot,
Living, and well; Son to Gentille, and Brother
To virtuous Casta; to your beauteous Mistriss,
The long since poor betroth'd, and still vow'd servant.

MARIA
Nay, sure he lives. My Lord Lavall, your Master,
Brought news long since to your much mourning Mistriss,
Ye dy'd at Orleance; bound her with an oath too,
To keep it secret from your aged Father,
Lest it should rack his heart.

PEROLOT
A pretty secret
To try my Mistriss Love, and make my welcome
From travel of more worth; from whence, Heaven be thanked,
My business for the Duke dispatch'd to th' purpose,
And all my money spent, I am come home, wench.
How does my Mistriss? for I have not yet seen
Any, nor will I, till I do her service.

MARIA
But did the Lord Laval know of your love, Sir, before he went?

PEROLOT
Yes, by much more force he got it,
But none else knew; upon his promise too
And honor to conceal it faithfully
Till my return; to further which, he told me,

My business being ended, from the Duke
He would procure a pension for my service,
Able to make my Mistriss a fit Husband.

MARIA
But are you sure of this?

PEROLOT
Sure as my sight, wench.

MARIA
Then is your Lord a base dissembling villain,
A Devil Lord, the damn'd Lord of all lewdness,
And has betraid ye, and undone my Mistriss,
My poor sweet Mistriss: oh that leacher Lord,
Who, poor soul, since was married.

PEROLOT
To whom, Maria?

MARIA
To that unlucky Lord, a pox upon him;
Whose hot horse-appetite being allaid once
With her chaste joyes, married again, scarce cool'd,
The Torches yet not out the yellow Hymen
Lighted about the bed, the Songs yet sounding,
Marine's young noble Daughter Helena,
Whose mischief stands at door next. Oh that recreant!

PEROLOT
Oh villain! Oh most unmanly falshood!
Nay then I see, my Letters were betraid too.
Oh, I am full of this, great with his mischiefs,
Loaden and burst: Come, lead me to my Lady.

MARIA
I cannot, Sir, L'avall keeps her conceal'd,
Besides, her griefs are such, she will see no man.

PEROLOT
I must, and will go to her: I will see her:
There be my friend, or this shall be thy furthest.

MARIA
Hold, and I'll help thee: but first ye shall swear to me,
As you are true and gentle, as ye hate
This beastly and base Lord, where I shall place ye,
(Which shall be within sight) till I discharge ye,

What-e'er you see or hear, to make no motion.

PEROLOT
I do by Heaven!

MARIA
Stay here about the house then,
Till it be later; yet the time's not perfect:
There at the back door I'll attend you truly.

PEROLOT
Oh monstrous, monstrous beastly villain.

[Exit.

MARIA
How cross this falls, and from all expectation!
And what the end shall be, Heaven only yet knows:
Only I wish, and hope. But I forget still,
Casta must be the bait, or all miscarries.

[Exeunt.

[Enter **GENTILLE** with a Torch, **SHALLOON** above.

GENTILLE
Holla, Shalloon.

SHALLOON
Who's there?

GENTILLE
A word from the Duke, Sir.

SHALLOON
Your pleasure.

GENTILLE
Tell your Lord he must to Court strait.

SHALLOON
He is ill at ease: and prays he may be pardon'd
The occasions of this night.

GENTILLE
Belike he is drunk then:
He must away; the Duke and his fair Lady,
The beauteous Helena, are now at Cent.

Of whom she has such fortune in her carding,
The Duke has lost a thousand Crowns, and swears,
He will not go to bed, till by Lavall
The Tide of loss be turn'd again. Awake him,
For 'tis the pleasure of the Duke he must rise.

SHALLOON
Having so strict command, Sir, to the contrary,
I dare not do it: I beseech your pardon.

GENTILLE
Are you sure he is there?

SHALLOON
Yes.

GENTILLE
And asleep?

SHALLOON
I think so.

GENTILLE
And are you sure you will not tell him, Shalon?

SHALLOON
Yes, very sure.

GENTILLE
Then I am sure, I will.
Open, or I must force.

SHALLOON
Pray ye stay, he is not,
Nor will not be this night. You may excuse it.

GENTILLE
I knew he was gone about some womans labour.
As good a neighbor, though I say it, and as comfortable:
Many such more we need Shalloon. Alas, poor Lady,
Thou art like to lie cross-legg'd to night. Good Monsieur,
I will excuse your Master for this once, Sir,
Because sometimes I have lov'd a wench my self too.

SHALLOON
'Tis a good hearing, Sir.

GENTILLE

But for your lye, Shalloon,
If I had you here, it should be no good hearing.
For your pate I would pummel.

SHALLOON
A fair good night, Sir.

GENTILLE
Good night, thou noble Knight, Sir Pandarus.
My heart is cold o'th' suddain, and a strange dulness
Possesses all my body: thy Will be done Heaven.

[Exit.

A Room in the House with a Gallery

[Enter **GABRIELLA** and **CASTA**: and **MARIA** with a Taper.

CASTA
'Faith Friend, I was even going to my bed,
When your Maid told me of your sudden sickness:
But from my grave (so truly I love you)
I think your name would raise me: ye look ill
Since last I saw ye, much decay'd in colour:
Yet I thank Heaven, I find no such great danger
As your Maid frighted me withal: take courage
And give your sickness course: some grief you have got
That feeds within upon your tender spirits,
And wanting open way to vent it self,
Murders your mind, and choaks up all your sweetness.

GABRIELLA
It was my Maids fault; worthy friend, to trouble ye,
So late, upon so light a cause: yet since I have ye
Oh my dear Casta.

CASTA
Out with it, God's name.

GABRIELLA
The Closset of my heart, I will lock here, wench,

[**L'AVALL** knocks within.

And things shall make ye tremble. Who's that knocks there?

MARIA
'Tis L'avall.

GABRIELLA
Sit you still. Let him in.
I am resolv'd, and all you wronged women,
You noble spirits, that as I have suffer'd
Under this glorious beast-insulting man,
Lend me your causes, then your cruelties,
For I must put on madness above women.

CASTA
Why do you look so ghastly?

GABRIELLA
Peace; no harm, Deer.

[Enter **L'AVALL**.

L'AVALL
There, take my cloak and sword: Where is this Banquet?

MARIA
In the next room.

CASTA
How came he here? Heaven bless me.

L'AVALL
Give me some Wine wench; fill it full, and sprightly.

GABRIELLA
Sit still, and be not fearful.

L'AVALL
Till my veins swell,
And my strong sinews stretch like that brave Centaur,
That at the Table snatch'd the Bride away
In spight of Hercules.

CASTA
I am betraid.

L'AVALL
Nay, start not Lady; 'tis for you that I come,
And for your beauty: 'tis for you, Lavall

Honors this night; to you, the sacred shrine
I humbly bow, offering my vows and prayers;
To you I live.

GABRIELLA
In with the powder quickly:
So, that and the Wine will rock ye.

L'AVALL
Here, to the health
Of the most beauteous and divine, fair Casta,
The star of sweetness.

GABRIELLA
Fear him not, I'll die first.
And who shall pledge ye?

L'AVALL
Thou shalt, thou tann'd Gipsey:
And worship to that brightness give, cold Tartar.
By Heaven ye shall not stir; ye are my Mistris,
The glory of my love, the great adventure,
The Mistris of my heart, and she my whore.

GABRIELLA
Thou ly'st, base, beastly Lord; drunker then anger,
Thou sowsed Lord, got by a surfeit, thou lyest basely.
Nay, stir not: I dare tell thee so. Sit you still.
If I be whore, it is in marrying thee,
That art so absolute and full a villain,
No Sacrament can save that piece tied to thee.
How often hast thou woo'd in those flatteries,
Almost those very words, my constancie?
What goddess have I not been, or what goodness
What star that is of any name in Heaven,
Or brightness? which of all the virtues
(But drunkenness, and drabbing, thy two morals)
Have not I reach'd to? what Spring was ever sweeter?
What Scythian snow so white? what crystal chaster?
Is not thy new wife now the same too? Hang thee,
Base Bigamist, thou honor of ill women.

CASTA
How's this? O! Heaven defend me.

GABRIELLA
Thou salt-itch,
For whom no cure but ever burning brimstone

Can be imagin'd.

L'AVALL
Ha, ha, ha.

GABRIELLA
Dost thou laugh, thou breaker
Of all law, all religion, of all faith
Thou Soule contemner?

L'AVALL
Peace, thou paltry woman:
And sit by me, Sweet.

GABRIELLA
By the Devil?

L'AVALL
Come,
And lull me with delights.

GABRIELLA
It works amain now.

L'AVALL
Give me such kisses as the Queen of shadows
Gave to the sleeping boy she stole on Latmus;
Look round about in snakie wreathes close folded,
Those rosie arms about my neck, O! Venus.

GABRIELLA
Fear not, I say.

L'AVALL
Thou admirable sweetness,
Distill thy blessings like those silver drops,
That falling on fair grounds, rise all in roses:
Shoot me a thousand darts from those fair eyes,
And through my heart transfix 'em all, I'll stand 'em.
Send me a thousand smiles, and presently
I'll catch 'em in mine eyes, and by Love's power
Turn 'em to Cupids all, and fling 'em on thee,
How high she looks, and heavenly! More wine for me.

GABRIELLA
Give him more wine, and good friend be not fearful.

L'AVALL

Here on my knee, thou Goddess of delights,
This lustie grape I offer to thy Beauties;
See how it leaps to view that perfect redness
That dwels upon thy lips: now, how it blushes
To be outblush'd. Oh! let me feed my fancie,
And as I hold the purple god in one hand
Dancing about the brim and proudly swelling,
Deck'd in the pride of nature young, and blowing;
So let me take fair Semele in the other,
And sing the loves of gods, then drink, their Nectar's
Not yet desir'd.

CASTA
Oh!

L'AVALL
Then like lustie Tarquin
Turn'd into flames with Lucrece coy denyals,
His blood and spirit equally ambitious,
I force thee for my own.

CASTA
O help me Justice:
Help me, my Chastitie.

L'AVALL
Now I am bravely quarried.

[**PEROLOT** above.

PEROLOT
'Tis my Sister.

GABRIELLA
No, bawdy slave, no Treacher, she is not carried.

PEROLOT
She's loose again, and gone. I'll keep my place still.

MARIA
Now it works bravely: stand, he cannot hurt ye.

L'AVALL
O my sweet Love, my life.

[He falls downe, and sleeps.

MARIA

He sinks.

L'AVALL
My blessing.

MARIA
So, now he is safe a while.

GABRIELLA
Lock all the doors, wench,
Then for my wrongs.

PEROLOT
Now I'll appear to know all.

GABRIELLA
Be quick, quick, good Marie, sure and sudden.

PEROLOT
Stay, I must in first.

GABRIELLA
O' my conscience!
It is young Perolot: Oh my stung conscience!
It is my first and noblest Love.

MARIA
Leave wondring,
And recollect your self: the man is living,
Equally wrong'd as you, and by that Devil.

PEROLOT
'Tis most true, Lady: your unhappy fortune
I grieve for as mine own, your fault forgive too,
If it be one. This is no time for kisses:
I have heard all, and known all, which mine ears
Are crack'd apieces with, and my heart perish'd.
I saw him in your chamber, saw his fury.
And am afire till I have found his heart out.
What do you mean to do? for I'll make one.

GABRIELLA
To make his death more horrid (for he shall dye).

PEROLOT
He must, he must.

GABRIELLA

We'll watch him till he wakes,
Then bind him, and then torture him.

PEROLOT
'Tis nothing.
No, take him dead drunk now without repentance,
His leachery inseam'd upon him.

GABRIELLA
Excellent.

PEROLOT
I'll do it my self; and when 'tis done, provide ye,
For we'll away for Italy this night.

GABRIELLA
We'll follow thorow all hazards.

PEROLOT
Oh false Lord,
Unmanly, mischievous; how I could curse thee;
But that but blasts thy fame; have at thy heart, fool:
Loop-holes I'll make enough to let thy life out.

L'AVALL
Oh! does the devil ride me?

PEROLOT
Nay then.

L'AVALL
Murder.
Nay, then take my share too.

PEROLOT
Help; oh! he has slain me.
Bloudy intentions must have bloud.

L'AVALL
Hah?

PEROLOT
Heaven.

GABRIELLA
He sinks, he sinks, for ever sinks: oh fortune!
Oh sorrow! how like seas thou flowest upon me!
Here will I dwell for ever. Weep Maria,

Weep this young man's misfortune: oh thou truest!

[Enter **SPIRIT**.

L'AVALL
What have I done?

SPIRIT
That that has mark'd thy soul man.

L'AVALL
And art thou come again thou dismal spirit?

SPIRIT
Yes, to devour thy last.

L'AVALL
Mercy upon thee.

SPIRIT
Thy hour is come: succession, honor, pleasure,
And all the lustre thou so long hast look'd for
Must here have end: Summon thy sins before thee.

L'AVALL
Oh my affrighted soul!

SPIRIT
There lies a black one;
Thy own best servant by thy own hand slain,
Thy drunkenness procur'd it: There's another:
Think of fair Gabriella, there she weeps;
And such tears are not lost.

L'AVALL
Oh miserable!

SPIRIT
Thy foul intention to the virtuous Casta.

L'AVALL
No more, no more, thou wild-fire.

SPIRIT
Last, thy last wife,
Think on the wrong she suffers.

L'AVALL

O my miserie.
Oh! whither shall I flie?

SPIRIT
Thou hast no faith, fool.
Heark to thy knell.

[Sings, and vanishes.

L'AVALL
Millions of sins muster about mine eyes now:
Murders, ambitions, lust, false faiths; O horror,
In what a stormie form of death thou rid'st now!
Me thinks I see all tortures, fires, and frosts,
Deep sinking caves, where nothing but despair dwels,
The balefull birds of night hovering about 'em;
A grave, me thinks, now opens, and a herse
Hung with my Arms tumbles into it: oh!
Oh! my afflicted soul: I cannot pray;
And the least child that has but goodness in him
May strike my head off; so stupid are my powers:
I'll lift mine eyes up though.

MARIA
Cease these laments,
They are too poor for vengence: L'avall lives yet.

GABRIELLA
Then thus I drie all sorrows from these eyes,
Fury and rage possess 'em now: damn'd divell.

L'AVALL
Hah?

GABRIELLA
This for young Perolot.

L'AVALL
O mercy, mercy.

GABRIELLA
This for my wrongs.

L'AVALL
But one short hour to cure me.

[Knock within.

Oh be not cruell: Oh! oh.

MARIA
Heark, they knock.
Make hast for Heavens sake, Mistris.

GABRIELLA
This for Casta.

L'AVALL
Oh, O, O, O!

[He dies.

MARIA
He's dead: come quickly, let's away with him,
'T will be too late else.

GABRIELLA
Help, help up to th' chamber!

[Exeunt with **L'AVALL'S** body.

[Enter **DUKE**, **HELLENA**, **GENTILLE**, **CASTA**, and **ATTENDANTS**, with lights.

DUKE
What frights are these?

GENTILLE
I am sure here 's one past frighting.
Bring the lights neerer: I have enough alreadie.
Out, out, mine eyes. Look, Casta.

LORD
'T is young Perolot.

DUKE
When came he over? Hold the Gentlewoman, she sinks; and bear her off.

CASTA
O my dear brother!

[Exit.

GENTILLE
There is a time for all; for me, I hope, too,
And very shortly. Murdred?

[**GABRIELLA**, **MARIA**, with **L'AVALL'S** body, above.

DUKE
Who's above there?

GABRIELLA
Look up, and see.

DUKE
What may this mean?

GABRIELLA
Behold it;
Behold the drunken murderer
Of that young Gentleman; behold the rankest,
The vilest, basest slave that ever flourish'd.

DUKE
Who kill'd him?

GABRIELLA
I; and there 's the cause I did it:
Read, if your eyes will give you leave.

HELLENA
Oh! monstrous.

GABRIELLA
Nay, out it shall: there, take this false heart to ye;
The base dishonor of a thousand women:
Keep it in gold, Duke, 'tis a precious jewel.
Now to my self; for I have liv'd a fair age,
Longer by some moneths then I had a mind to.

DUKE
Hold.

GABRIELLA
Here, young Perolot; my first contracted
True love shall never go alone.

DUKE
Hold, Gabriella.
I do forgive all.

GABRIELLA
I shall die the better,
Thus let me seek my grave, and my shames with me.

MARIA
Nor shalt thou go alone my noble Mistris:
Why should I live, and thou dead?

LORD
Save the wench there.

MARIA
She is, I hope; and all my sins here written.

DUKE
This was a fatal night.

GENTILLE
Heaven has his working,
Which we cannot contend against.

DUKE
Alas!

GENTILLE
Your Grace has your alas too.

DUKE
Would 't were equal;
For thou hast lost an honest noble childe.

GENTILLE
'T is heir enough has lost a good remembrance.

DUKE
See all their bodies buried decently,
Though some deserv'd it not. How do you, Lady?

HELLENA
Even with your Graces leave, ripe for a Monasterie;
There will I wed my life to tears and prayers,
And never know what man is more.

DUKE
Your pleasure;
How does the maid within?

LORD
She is gone before, Sir,
The same course that my Lady takes.

GENTILLE
And my course shall be my Beads at home; so
Please your Grace to give me leave to leave the Court.

DUKE
In peace, Sir,
And take my love along.

GENTILLE
I shall pray for ye.

DUKE
Now to our selves retire we, and begin
By this example to correct each sin.

[Exeunt.

[Flourish.

KING EMANUEL
By this we plainly view the two imposthumes
That choke a kingdoms welfare; Ease, and Wantonness;
In both of which Lavall was capital:
For first, Ease stole away his minde from honor,
That active noble thoughts had kept still working,
And then deliver'd him to drink and women,
Lust and outragious riot; and what their ends are,
How infamous and foul, we see example.
Therefore, that great man that will keep his name,
And gain his merit out of Virtues schools,
Must make the pleasures of the world his fools.

[Flourish.

THE TRIUMPH OF TIME

SCENE I

A City

[Enter **MUSICIANS**: next them, **PEROLOT** with the wound he died with. Then **GABRIELLA** and **MARIA**, with their wounds: after them, **FOUR FURIES** with Bannerets inscrib'd Revenge, Murder, Lust and Drunkenness, singing. Next them, **L'AVALL** wounded. Then a Chariot with **DEATH** drawn by the **DESTINIES**.

[Flourish.

[Enter **PROLOGUE**.

From this sad sight ascend your noble eye,
And see old Time helping triumphantly,
Helping his Master Man: view here his vanities
And see his false friends like those glutted flyes,
That when they've suckt their fill, fall off, and fade
From all remembrance of him, like a shade.
And last, view who relieves him; and that gone,
We hope your favour, and our Play is done.

[Flourish.

[Enter **ANTHROPOS**, **DESIRE**, and **VAIN DELIGHT**; **BOUNTY**.

ANTHROPOS
What hast thou done, Desire, and how imploy'd
The charge I gave thee, about levying wealth
For our supplies?

DESIRE
I have done all, yet nothing:
Tri'd all, and all my ways, yet all miscarried;
There dwells a sordid dulness in their mindes
Thou son of earth, colder then that thou art made of,
I came to Craft, found all his hooks about him,
And all his nets baited and set; his slie self
And greedie Lucre at a serious conference
Which way to tie the world within their statutes:
Business of all sides and of all sorts swarming
Like Bees broke loose in summer: I declared
Your will and want together, both inforcing
With all the power and pains I had, to reach him;
Yet all fell short.

ANTHROPOS
His answer.

DESIRE
This he gave me.
Your wants are never ending; and those supplies
That came to stop those breaches, are ever lavisht
Before they reach the main, in toys and trifles,
Gew-gaws, and gilded puppets: Vain delight
He says has ruin'd ye, with clapping all
That comes in for support, on clothes, and Coaches,
Perfumes, and powder'd pates; and that your Mistris,

The Lady Pleasure, like a sea devours
At length both you and him too. If you have houses,
Or land, or jewels, for good pawn, he'll hear you,
And will be readie to supplie occasions;
If not, he locks his ears up, and grows stupid.
From him, I went to Vanity, whom I found
Attended by an endless troop of Tailors,
Mercers, Embroiderers, Feather-makers, Fumers,
All occupations opening like a Mart,
That serve to rig the body out with braverie;
And th'row the roome new fashions flew like flyes,
In thousand gaudie shapes; Pride waiting on her,
And busily surveying all the breaches
Time and delaying Nature had wrought in her,
Which still with art she piec'd again, and strengthened:
I told your wants; she shew'd me gowns and head-tires,
Imbroider'd wastcoats, smocks seam'd thorow with cut-works,
Scarfs, mantles, petticoats, muffs, powders, paintings,
Dogs, monkeys, parrots, which all seemed to shew me
The way her money went. From her to Pleasure
I took my journey.

ANTHROPOS
And what says our best Mistris?

DESIRE
She danc'd me out this answer presently:
Revels and Masques had drawn her drie alreadie.
I met old Time too, mowing mankind down,
Who says you are too hot, and he must purge ye.

ANTHROPOS
A cold quietus. Miserable creatures,
Born to support and beautifie your master,
The godlike man, set here to do me service,
The children of my will; why, or how dare ye,
Created to my use alone, disgrace me?
Beasts have more courtesie; they live about me,
Offering their warm wooll to the shearers hand,
To clothe me with their bodies to my labours;
Nay, even their lives they daily sacrifice,
And proudly press with garlands to the altars,
To fill the gods oblations. Birds bow to me,
Striking their downie sails to do me service,
Their sweet airs ever ecchoing to mine honor,
And to my rest their plumie softs they send me.
Fishes, and plants, and all where life inhabits,
But mine own cursed kind, obey their ruler;

Mine have forgot me, miserable mine,
Into whose stonie hearts, neglect of dutie,
Squint-ey'd deceit, and self-love, are crept closely:
None feel my wants, not one mend with me.

DESIRE
None, Sir?

ANTHROPOS
Thou hast forgot (Desire) thy best friend, Flatterie;
He cannot fail me.

DELIGHT
Fail? he will sell himself,
And all within his power, close to his skin first.

DESIRE
I thought so too, and made him my first venture
But found him in a young Lords ear so busie,
So like a smiling showr pouring his soul
In at his portals, his face in a thousand figures
Catching the vain mind of the men: I pull'd him,
But still he hung like birdlime; spoke unto him,
His answer still was, By the Lord, sweet Lord,
And By my soul, thou master-piece of honor;
Nothing could stave him off: he has heard your flood's gone;
And on decaying things he seldom smiles, Sir.

ANTHROPOS
Then here I break up state, and free my followers,
Putting my fortune now to Time, and Justice:
Go seek new masters now; for Anthropos
Neglected by his friends, must seek new fortunes.
Desire, to Avarice I here commend thee,
Where thou may'st live at full bent of thy wishes:
And Vain Delight, thou feeder of my follies
With light fantastickness, be thou in favour.
To leave thee, Bountie, my most worthie servant,
Troubles me more then mine own misery;
But we must part: go plant thy self, my best friend,
In honorable hearts that truely know thee,
And there live ever like thy self, a virtue:
But leave this place, and seek the Countrey,
For Law, and lust, like fire lick all up here.
Now none but Poverty must follow me,
Despis'd patch'd Poverty; and we two married,
Will seek Simplicity, Content and Peace out.

[Enter **POVERTY**.

And live with them in exile. How uncall'd on
My true friend comes!

POVERTY
Here, hold thee, Anthropos,
Thou art almost arm'd at rest; put this on,
A penitential robe, to purge thy pleasures:
Off with that vanitie.

ANTHROPOS
Here, Vain Delight,
And with this all my part, to thee again
Of thee I freely render.

POVERTY
Take this staff now,
And be more constant to your steps hereafter:
The staff is Staidness of affections.
Away you painted flyes, that with mans summet
Take life and heat buzzing about his blossoms;
When growing full, ye turn to Caterpillers,
Gnawing the root that gave you life. Fly shadows.

[Exeunt **DESIRE** and **DELIGHT**.

Now to Content I'll give thee, Anthropos,
To Rest and Peace: no vanitie dwells there;
Desire nor Pleasure, to delude thy mind more;
No Flatteries smooth-fil'd tongue shall poison thee.

ANTHROPOS
O! Jupiter, if I have ever offer'd
Upon thy burning Altars but one Sacrifice
Thou and thy fair-ey'd Juno smil'd upon;
If ever, to thine honor, bounteous feasts,
Where all thy statues sweet with wine and incense,
Have by the son of earth been celebrated:
Hear me (the child of shame now) hear thou helper,
And take my wrongs into thy hands, thou justice
Done by unmindful man, unmerciful,
Against his master done, against thy order;
And raise again, thou father of all honor,
The poor despis'd, but yet thy noblest creature.
Raise from his ruines once more this sunk Cedar,
That all may fear thy power, and I proclaim it.

[Exeunt.

Olympus

[JUPITER and MERCURY descend severally. Trumpets small above.

JUPITER
Ho! Mercury, my winged son.

MERCURY
Your servant.

JUPITER
Whose powerful prayers were those that reach'd our ears,
Arm'd in such spells of pity now?

MERCURY
The sad petitions
Of the scorn'd son of earth, the god-like Anthropos,
He that has swell'd your sacred fires with incense,
And pil'd upon your Altars a thousand heifers;
He that (beguil'd by Vanity and Pleasure,
Desire, Craft, Flattery, and smooth Hypocrisie)
Stands now despis'd and ruin'd, left to Poverty.

JUPITER
It must not be; he was not rais'd for ruine;
Nor shall those hands heav'd at mine Altars, perish:
He is our noblest creature. Flee to Time,
And charge him presently release the bands
Of Poverty and Want this suitor sinks in:
Tell him, among the Sun-burnt Indians,
That know no other wealth but Peace and pleasure,
She shall find golden Plutus, god of riches,
Who idly is ador'd, the innocent people
Not knowing yet what power and weight he carries:
Bid him compell him to his right use, honor,
And presently to live with Anthropos.
It is our Will. Away.

MERCURY
I do obey it.

[JUPITER and MERCURY ascend again.

A Savage Country

[Musick. Enter **PLUTUS**, with a troop of **INDIANS**, singing and dancing wildly about him, and bowing to him: which ended, Enter **TIME**.

TIME
Rise, and away; 'tis Joves command.

PLUTUS
I will not:
Ye have some fool to furnish now; some Midas
That to no purpose I must choak with riches.
Who must I go to?

TIME
To the son of earth;
He wants the god of wealth.

PLUTUS
Let him want still:
I was too lately with him, almost torn
Into ten thousand pieces by his followers:
I could not sleep, but Craft or Vanity
Were filing off my fingers; not eat, for fear
Pleasure would cast her self into my belly,
And there surprize my heart.

TIME
These have forsaken him:
Make haste then, thou must with me: be not angry,
For fear a greater anger light upon thee.

PLUTUS
I do obey then: but change my figure;
For when I willingly befriend a creature,
Goodly, and full of glory I shew to him;
But when I am compell'd, old, and decrepid,
I halt, and hang upon my staff. Farewell, friends,
I will not be long from ye; all my servants
I leave among ye still, and my chief riches.

[Exeunt **INDIANS** with a dance.

Oh Time, what innocence dwells here, what goodness!
They know me not, nor hurt me not, yet hug me.
Away, I'll follow thee: but not too fast, Time.

[Exeunt **PLUTUS** and **TIME**.

A Rocky Country

[Enter **ANTHROPOS, HONESTY, SIMPLICITY, HUMILITY, POVERTY.**

HUMILITY
Man, be not sad, nor let this divorce
From Mundus, and his many ways of pleasure,
Afflict thy spirits; which consider'd rightly
With inward eyes, makes thee arrive at happy.

POVERTY
For now what danger or deceit can reach thee?
What matter left for Craft or Covetize
To plot against thee? what Desire to burn thee?

HONESTY
Oh son of earth, let Honesty possess thee;
Be as thou wast intended, like thy Maker;
See thorow those gawdy shadows, that like dreams
Have dwelt upon thee long: call up thy goodness,
Thy mind and man within thee, that lie shipwrack'd,
And then how thin and vain these fond affections,
How lame this worldly love, how lump-like raw
And ill digested all these vanities
Will shew, let Reason tell thee.

SIMPLICITY
Crown thy mind
With that above the worlds wealth, joyful suff'ring,
And truly be the master of thy self.
Which is the noblest Empire; and there stand
The thing thou wert ordain'd, and set to govern.

POVERTY
Come, let us sing the worlds shame: hear us, Anthropos.

[Song: And then Enter **TIME** and **PLUTUS**.

HONESTY
Away; we are betrayd.

[Exeunt all but **POVERTY**.

TIME
Get thou too after,
Thou needy bare companion; go for ever,
For ever, I conjure thee: make no answer.

[Exit **POVERTY**.

ANTHROPOS
What mak'st thou here, Time? thou that to this Minute,
never stood still by me?

TIME
I have brought thee succour;
And now catch hold, I am thine: The god of riches
(Compell'd by him that saw thy miseries,
The ever just and wakeful Jove, at length)
Is come unto thee: use him as thine own;
For 'tis the doom of Heaven: he must obey thee.

ANTHROPOS
Have I found pity then?

TIME
Thou hast; and Justice
Against those false seducers of thine honor:
Come, give him present helps.

[Exit **TIME**.

[**INDUSTRY** and the **ARTS** discovered.

PLUTUS
Come Industry,
Thou friend of life; and next to thee, rise Labour;

[**PLUTUS** stamps. **LABOUR** rises.

Rise presently: and now to your employments;
But first conduct this mortal to the rock.

[They carry **ANTHROPOS** to a Rock, and fall a digging.

What seest thou now?

[**PLUTUS** strikes the Rock, and flames flie out.

ANTHROPOS
A glorious Mine of Metal.
Oh Jupiter, my thanks.

PLUTUS
To me a little.

ANTHROPOS
And to the god of wealth, my Sacrifice.

PLUTUS
Nay, then I am rewarded. Take heed now, Son,
You are afloat again, lest Mundus catch ye.

ANTHROPOS
Never betray me more.

PLUTUS
I must to India,
From whence I came, where my main wealth lies buried,
And these must with me. Take that Book and Mattock,
And by those, know to live again.

[Exeunt **PLUTUS**, **INDUSTRY**, **LABOUR**, &c.

ANTHROPOS
I shall do.

[Enter **FAME** sounding.

FAME
Thorow all the world, the fortune of great Anthropos
Be known and wonder'd at; his riches envy'd
As far as Sun or Time is; his power fear'd too.

[Exeunt.

[MUSICK.

[Enter **DELIGHT**, **PLEASURE**, **CRAFT**, **LUCRE**, **VANITY**, &c. dancing and Masqu'd towards the Rock,
offering service to **ANTHROPHOS**. **MERCURY** from above. Musick heard. One half of a cloud drawn.
SINGERS are discovered: then the other half drawn. **JUPITER** seen in glory.

MERCURY
Take heed, weak man, those are the sins that sunk thee:

Trust 'em no more: kneel, and give thanks to Jupiter.

ANTHROPOS
Oh mighty power!

JUPITER
Unmask, ye gilded poisons:
Now look upon 'em, son of earth, and shame 'em;
Now see the faces of thy evil Angels,
Lead 'em to Time, and let 'em fill his Triumph:
Their memories be here forgot for ever.

ANTHROPOS
Oh just great god! how many lives of service,
What ages only given to thine honor.
What infinites of vows, and holy prayers,
Can pay my thanks?

JUPITER
Rise up: and to assure thee
That never more thou shalt feel want, strike, Mercury,
Strike him; and by that stroke he shall for ever
Live in that rock of Gold, and still enjoy it.
Be't done, I say. Now sing in honor of him.

[SONG.

[Enter the Triumph. First, the **MUSICIANS**: then **VAIN DELIGHT**, **PLEASURE**, **CRAFT**, **LUCRE**, **VANITY**, and other of the **VICES**: Then a Chariot with the person of **TIME** sitting in it, drawn by **FOUR PERSONS**, representing **HOURS**, singing.

[Exeunt.

[Flourish.

KING EMANUEL
By this we note (sweet-heart) in Kings and Princes
A weakness, even in spite of all their wisdoms.
And often to be master'd by abuses:
Our natures here describ'd too, and what humors
Prevail above our Reasons to undo us.
But this the last and best. When no friend stands,
The gods are merciful, and lend their hands.

[Flourish.

EPILOGUE

Now as the Husbandman, whose Costs and Pain,
Whose Hopes and Helps lie buried in his Grain,
Waiting a happy Spring to ripen full
His long'd-for Harvest, to the Reapers pull;
Stand we expecting, having sown our Ground
With so much charge, (the fruitfulness not found)
The Harvest of our Labours: For we know
You are our Spring; and when you smile, we grow.
Nor Charge nor Pain, shall bind us from your Pleasures,
So you but lend your hands to fill our Measures.

John Fletcher – A Short Biography

John Fletcher was born in December, 1579 in Rye, Sussex. He was baptised on December 20th.

As can be imagined details of much of his life and career have not survived and, accordingly, only a very brief indication of his life and works can be given.

His father, Richard Fletcher, was a successful and rather ambitious cleric. From being the Dean of Peterborough he moved on to become the Bishop of Bristol, Bishop of Worcester and finally, shortly before his death, the Bishop of London. He was also the chaplain to Queen Elizabeth.

When he was Dean of Peterborough, Richard Fletcher, witnessed the execution of Mary, Queen of Scots. It was said he "knelt down on the scaffold steps and started to pray out loud and at length, in a prolonged and rhetorical style, as though determined to force his way into the pages of history". He cried out at her death, "So perish all the Queen's enemies!" All very dramatic but the family did have strong links to the Arts.

Young Fletcher appears at the very young age of eleven to have entered Corpus Christi College at Cambridge University in 1591. There are no records that he ever took a degree but there is some small evidence that he was being prepared for a career in the church.

However what is clear is that this was soon abandoned as he joined the stream of people who would leave University and decamp to the more bohemian life of commercial theatre in London.

Unfortunately his father fell out with Queen Elizabeth but appears to have been on his way to rehabilitation before his death in 1596. At his death he was, however, mired in debt.

The upbringing of the now teenage Fletcher and his seven siblings now passed to his paternal uncle, the poet and minor official Giles Fletcher. Giles, who had the patronage of the Earl of Essex may have been a liability rather than an advantage to the young Fletcher. With Essex involved in the failed rebellion against Elizabeth Giles was also tainted by association.

By 1606 John Fletcher appears to have equipped himself with the talents to become a playwright. Initially this appears to have been for the Children of the Queen's Revels, then performing at the Blackfriars Theatre.

Commendatory verses by Richard Brome in the Beaumont and Fletcher 1647 folio place Fletcher in the company of Ben Jonson, although it is not known when this friendship began. Jonson, of course, was a leviathan of English Literature, so admired that many of his literary friends and colleagues were simply known as 'Sons of Ben'. Fletcher's frequent early collaborator, Francis Beaumont, was also a friend of Jonson's.

Fletcher's early career was marked by one significant failure; The Faithful Shepherdess, his adaptation of Giovanni Battista Guarini's Il Pastor Fido, which was performed by the Blackfriars Children in 1608. In the preface to the printed edition of his play, Fletcher explained the failure as due to his audience's faulty expectations. They expected a pastoral tragicomedy to feature dances, comedy, and murder, with the shepherds presented in conventional stereotypes – as Fletcher put it, wearing "gray cloaks, with curtailed dogs in strings." Fletcher's preface is however best known for its pithy definition of tragicomedy: "A tragicomedy is not so called in respect of mirth and killing, but in respect it wants [i.e., lacks] deaths, which is enough to make it no tragedy; yet brings some near it, which is enough to make it no comedy." A comedy, he went on to say, must be "a representation of familiar people." His preface is critical of drama that features characters whose action violates nature.

In that case, Fletcher appears to have been developing a new style faster than audiences could comprehend. By 1609, however, he had found his stride. With Beaumont, he wrote Philaster, which became a hit for the King's Men and began a profitable association between Fletcher and that company. Philaster appears also to have begun a trend for tragicomedy. Fletcher's influence has also been said to have inspired some features of Shakespeare's late romances, and certainly his influence on the tragicomic work of other playwrights is even more marked.

By the middle of the 1610s, Fletcher's plays had achieved a popularity that rivalled Shakespeare's and cemented the pre-eminence of the King's Men in Jacobean London. After Beaumont's retirement, necessitated by ill-health, and then his early death in 1616, Fletcher continued working, both singly and in collaboration, until his death in 1625. By that time, he had produced, or had been credited with, close to fifty plays. This body of work remained a major part of the King's Men's repertory until the closing of the theatres in 1642 due to the Civil War.

At the beginning of his career Fletcher's most important collaborator was Francis Beaumont. The two wrote together for close to a decade, first for the Children of the Queen's Revels, and then for the King's Men. According to an anecdote transmitted or invented by John Aubrey, they also lived together in Bankside, sharing clothes and having "one wench in the house between them." This domestic arrangement, if it existed, was ended by Beaumont's marriage in 1613, and their dramatic partnership ended after Beaumont fell ill, probably of a stroke, that same year.

At this point Fletcher had written many plays with Beaumont and several others on his own. He seems to have been regarded as quite a talent although it should be remembered that playwrights were required to be prolific, to easily work with other collaborators and to produce work of quality and commercial appeal very quickly.

The King's Men, run by Philip Henslowe, was the most prestigious of the theatre companies and Fletcher now had an increasingly close association with it.

Fletcher collaborated with Shakespeare on Henry VIII, The Two Noble Kinsmen, and the now lost Cardenio, which some scholars say was the basis for Lewis Theobald's play Double Falsehood. (Theobald is regarded as one of the best Shakespearean editors. Whether his play is based on Cardenio or on some other is not absolutely known although Theobald certainly promoted it as his revision of the lost Shakespeare/Fletcher play.)

A play that Fletcher also wrote by himself at this time, The Woman's Prize or the Tamer Tamed, is also regarded as a sequel to The Taming of the Shrew.

In 1616, with the death of Shakespeare, Fletcher now appears to have entered into an enhanced arrangement with the King's Men on very similar terms to Shakespeare's. Fletcher would now write exclusively for the King's Men until his own death almost a decade later.

As well as continuing his solo productions Fletcher was still collaborating with other playwrights, mainly Philip Massinger, who, in turn, would succeed him as the in-house playwright for the King's Men.

Fletcher's popularity continued throughout his life; indeed during the winter of 1621, he had three of his plays performed at court. His mastery is most notable in two dramatic types; tragicomedy and the comedy of manners.

John Fletcher died in 1625, it is thought of bubonic plague which, at the time, was undergoing further outbreaks.

He seems to have been buried in what is now Southwark Cathedral, although a precise location is not known. There is much made of an anecdote that Fletcher and Massinger (who died in 1640) share the same grave but it is more likely that both are buried within a few yards of each other and that the stone markers in the floor have confused the issue. One is marked 'Edmond Shakespeare 1607' and the other 'John Fletcher 1625' refers to Shakespeare's younger brother and the playwright. The churchyards were, more often than not, completely over-crowded and breeding grounds for disease. Precise record keeping was not a practiced skill.

During the later Commonwealth, many of the playwright's best-known scenes were kept alive as drolls. These were brief performances, usually condensed into one or two scenes and with the addition of music or song to satisfy the taste for plays while the theatres were closed under the Puritans. At the re-opening of the theatres in 1660, the plays in the Fletcher canon, in original form or revised, were by far the most common productions on the English stage. The most frequently revived plays suggest the developing taste for comedies of manners. Among the tragedies, The Maid's Tragedy and, especially, Rollo Duke of Normandy held the stage. Four tragicomedies (A King and No King, The Humorous Lieutenant, Philaster, and The Island Princess) were popular, perhaps in part for their similarity to and foreshadowing of heroic drama. Four comedies (Rule a Wife And Have a Wife, The Chances, Beggars' Bush, and especially The Scornful Lady) were also stage mainstays.

Despite his popularity, and it appears he was held in higher regard than Shakespeare at this time, his works steadily lost ground to those of Shakespeare and to new productions from other playwrights.

Since then Fletcher has increasingly become a subject only for occasional revivals and for specialists. Fletcher and his collaborators have been the subject of important bibliographic and critical studies, but the plays have been revived only infrequently.

Due to the frequent collaborations between all manner of playwrights, and the revisions carried out in later years, having a settled list of authorship to any given set of plays can be problematic. The works of Fletcher and others of this period most definitely fall into this category. It is as well to take into account that during this period theatres were quite often closed either due to outbreaks of the plague or to the prevailing political and moral climate. Printers, anxious to provide materials that would sell, were not above changing a name or two to enhance sales.

Although Fletcher collaborated most often with Beaumont and Massinger, it is believed that Massinger revised many of the plays some time after their original production. Other collaborators including Nathan Field, William Shakespeare, William Rowley and others also can be seen distinctly in Fletchers' works. Many modern scholars point out that Fletcher had many particular mannerisms but other playwrights would also duplicate these at times so allocating exact contributions of anyone to a play is somewhat of a detective case in many instances. However from the original folio printings or licensing via the Master of the Revels (the statutory licensing authority to approve and censor plays as well a hand in publication and printing of theatrical materials) as well as contemporary notes a fairly precise bibliography of the works can be given with only a few plays lacking substantial authority and provenance.

John Fletcher – A Concise Bibliography

This bibliography gives the most likely date of writing together with when published, revised or licensed by the Master or the Revels (This position within the royal household was originally for royal festivities, ie revels, and later to oversee stage censorship, until this function was transferred to the Lord Chamberlain in 1624).

Solo Plays
The Faithful Shepherdess, pastoral (written 1608–9; printed 1609)
The Tragedy of Valentinian, tragedy (1610–14; 1647)
Monsieur Thomas, comedy (c. 1610–16; 1639)
The Woman's Prize, or The Tamer Tamed, comedy (c. 1611; 1647)
Bonduca, tragedy (1611–14; 1647)
The Chances, comedy (c. 1613–25; 1647)
Wit Without Money, comedy (c. 1614; 1639)
The Mad Lover, tragicomedy (acted 5 January 1617; 1647)
The Loyal Subject, tragicomedy (licensed 16 November 1618; revised 1633; 1647)
The Humorous Lieutenant, tragicomedy (c. 1619; 1647)
Women Pleased, tragicomedy (c. 1619–23; 1647)
The Island Princess, tragicomedy (c. 1620; 1647)
The Wild Goose Chase, comedy (c. 1621; 1652)
The Pilgrim, comedy (c. 1621; 1647)
A Wife for a Month, tragicomedy (licensed 27 May 1624; 1647)
Rule a Wife and Have a Wife, comedy (licensed 19 October 1624; 1640)

Collaborations

With Francis Beaumont
The Woman Hater, comedy (1606; 1607)
Cupid's Revenge, tragedy (c. 1607–12; 1615)
Philaster, or Love Lies a-Bleeding, tragicomedy (c. 1609; 1620)
The Maid's Tragedy, Tragedy (c. 1609; 1619)
A King and No King, tragicomedy (1611; 1619)
The Captain, comedy (c. 1609–12; 1647)
The Scornful Lady, comedy (c. 1613; 1616)
Love's Pilgrimage, tragicomedy (c. 1615–16; 1647)
The Noble Gentleman, comedy (c. 1613; licensed 3 February 1626; 1647)

With Francis Beaumont & Philip Massinger
Thierry & Theodoret, tragedy (c. 1607; 1621)
The Coxcomb, comedy (c. 1608–10; 1647)
Beggars' Bush, comedy (c. 1612–13; revised 1622; 1647)
Love's Cure, comedy (c. 1612–13; revised 1625; 1647)

With Philip Massinger
Sir John van Olden Barnavelt, tragedy (August 1619; MS)
The Little French Lawyer, comedy (c. 1619–23; 1647)
A Very Woman, tragicomedy (c. 1619–22; licensed 6 June 1634; 1655)
The Custom of the Country, comedy (c. 1619–23; 1647)
The Double Marriage, tragedy (c. 1619–23; 1647)
The False One, history (c. 1619–23; 1647)
The Prophetess, tragicomedy (licensed 14 May 1622; 1647)
The Sea Voyage, comedy (licensed 22 June 1622; 1647)
The Spanish Curate, comedy (licensed 24 October 1622; 1647)
The Lovers' Progress or The Wandering Lovers, tragicomedy (licensed 6 December 1623; rev 1634; 1647)
The Elder Brother, comedy (c. 1625; 1637)

With Philip Massinger & Nathan Field
The Honest Man's Fortune, tragicomedy (1613; 1647)
The Queen of Corinth, tragicomedy (c. 1616–18; 1647)
The Knight of Malta, tragicomedy (c. 1619; 1647)

With William Shakespeare
Henry VIII, history (c. 1613; 1623)
The Two Noble Kinsmen, tragicomedy (c. 1613; 1634)
Cardenio, tragicomedy (c. 1613)

With Thomas Middleton & William Rowley
Wit at Several Weapons, comedy (c. 1610–20; 1647)

With William Rowley

The Maid in the Mill (licensed 29 August 1623; 1647).

Four Plays, or Moral Representations, in One, morality (c. 1608–13; 1647)

Rollo Duke of Normandy, or The Bloody Brother, tragedy (c. 1617; revised 1627–30; 1639)

The Night Walker, or The Little Thief, comedy (c. 1611; 1640)
The Coronation c. 1635

The Nice Valour, or The Passionate Madman, comedy (c. 1615–25; 1647)
The Laws of Candy, tragicomedy (c. 1619–23; 1647)
The Fair Maid of the Inn, comedy (licensed 22 January 1626; 1647)
The Faithful Friends, tragicomedy (registered 29 June 1660; MS.)

The Nice Valour is possibly by Fletcher revised by Thomas Middleton;

The Fair Maid of the Inn is perhaps a play by Massinger, John Ford, and John Webster, either with or without Fletcher's involvement.

The Laws of Candy has been variously attributed to Fletcher and to John Ford.

The Night-Walker was a Fletcher original, with additions by Shirley for a 1639 production.

Even now there is not absolute certainty on several of the plays. The first Beaumont & Fletcher folio of 1647 contained 35 plays and the second folio of 1679 added a further 18. In total 53 plays.

The first folio included The Masque of the Inner Temple and Gray's Inn (1613), and the second The Knight of the Burning Pestle (1607), widely considered Beaumont's solo works, although the latter was in early editions attributed to both writers. Fletcher himself said that Beaumont was attributed so-authorship of many works that belonged solely to Fletcher or to other collaborators.

One play in the canon, Sir John Van Olden Barnavelt, existed in manuscript and was not published till 1883.

Nathan Field was born on 17th October 1587 or baptized on October 17, 1587, unfortunately accounts vary as to which.

He was the youngest of seven children, to John and Joan Field. Intriguingly Nathan's father, a Purtian preacher, was very much opposed to London's public entertainments. A sermon he delivered attributed Divine judgment to several deaths during a bear baiting on a Sunday, at Beargarden in 1583.

When Nathan was only a few months old his father died in March, 1588. Now his mother Joan was tasked with bringing up the 7 children by herself.

However, after attending St Paul School in the late 1590's he seems, on or around 1600, to have impressed Nathaniel Giles, the master of the Children of the Chapel Royal and also a manager of the new troupe of boy players at Blackfriars Theatre.

Nathan would now remain in theatre for the rest of his young life.

As a member of the Children of the Queen's Revels, Field acted in the innovative drama staged at Blackfriars in the early 1600's. Cast lists associate him with Ben Jonson's Cynthia's Revels (1600) and The Poetaster (1601); a 1641 quarto also associates him with George Chapman's Bussy D'Ambois.

Later in the decade, he performed in Jonson's Epicoene and, it is thought, played Humphrey in Francis Beaumont's The Knight of the Burning Pestle. During the same years, he wrote commendatory verses for Jonson's Volpone and Catiline, as well as John Fletcher's The Faithful Shepherdess.

It is thought that Field was also among several of the theatre company briefly imprisoned for the official displeasure brought about by performances of both Eastward Hoe, authored by Jonson, Chapman & Marston, and John Day's The Isle of Gulls; the latter imprisonment was in Bridewell Prison.

Field stayed with the children's company until 1613, his twenty-sixth year. He appears to be the only one of the boy actors of 1600 to remain with the Blackfriars troupe when, in 1609, Philip Rosseter and Robert Keysar assumed control of the company. In this company, he performed in the theatre in Whitefriars and, frequently, at court, in plays such as Beaumont and Fletcher's The Coxcomb.

By this time Field had also added playwright to his talents. His first was A Woman is a Weathercock. This would lead to collaborators with some of the very best and most highly regarded dramatists of their day.

In 1613, Rosseter combined his company with the Lady Elizabeth's Men, managed by the Elizabethan entrepreneur Philip Henslowe. Performing at the Swan Theatre and Hope Theatre, Field acted in Thomas Middleton's A Chaste Maid in Cheapside and Jonson's Bartholomew Fair.

These years witnessed some degree of tumult; Henslowe's business practices resulted in his actors' drawing up certain "articles of grievance" against him, and Rosseter's attempt to build a new private theatre, Porter's Hall, in Blackfriars.

This period ended with the death of Henslowe and Rosseter abandoning his plans after they were turned down by both the city and Privy Council. The Lady Elizabeth's Men briefly merged and then separated from Prince Charles's Men, thereafter were touring in the country.

For Field, the period had a more satisfactory end: by late 1616, he had joined the King's Men, possibly, it is believed, to replace Shakespeare as actor. His name appears on the list of actors given in the First Folio of Shakespeare's plays in 1623. He was said to be an outstanding actor.

With the King's Men, Field seems to have performed as Voltore in Volpone and as Face in The Alchemist. It is not clear what other parts he played. Of course, he acted in a number of Fletcher's plays, as well as

Shakespeare's; presumably he also acted in his own Amends for Ladies (printed 1618, though probably written earlier), and in The Fatal Dowry, which he wrote with Philip Massinger.

However, set against this was his bohemian lifestyle which was notoriously wild. The gossip of the day reported that Field was forced to quit the stage after a scandal in 1619 when he fathered a child by the Countess of Argyll. In 1619 a pamphlet circulated stating that the Earl of Argyll had paid "for the nursing of a child which the world says is a daughter to my lady and N. Field the Player."

Nathan Field died at some point between May 1619 and August 1620. By then he was still only in his early thirties but had made a distinctive contribution to the era's theatre.

Nathan Field – A Concise Bibliography

In common with many other playwrights of the era works were frequently made in collaboration with one or more others. Credits were often mis-attributed of not given at all. Modern scholars have made a great effort to untangle the authors of this period and, whilst not a complete list of his works, it gives a very good indication of his canon.

A Woman Is a Weathercock (A Comedy, acted circa 1609, printed 1612)
Amends for Ladies (A Comedy, acted by 1611, printed 1618)
The Fatal Dowry (circa 1619, printed 1632) with Philip Massinger
Four Plays, or Moral Representations, in One (circa 1608–13 printed 1647) with John Fletcher
The Honest Man's Fortune (MS 1613 printed 1647) with John Fletcher & Philip Massinger
The Queen of Corinth (circa 1616, printed 1647) with John Fletcher & Philip Massinger
The Knight of Malta (circa 1616-19, printed 1647)

www.ingramcontent.com/pod-product-compliance
Lightning Source LLC
Chambersburg PA
CBHW060120050426
42448CB00010B/1961